JASON WEBER

TRAIN TOUGH

GO **HARD** OR GO HOME

ABC
Books

TO MY FATHER JOHN FOR PUTTING ME ON THE PATH.

TO MY MOTHER HELEN FOR KEEPING ME ON THE PATH.

TO MY BEAUTIFUL WIFE SUSE AND OUR CHILDREN ABBY AND BEN FOR MAKING THE PATH WORTH TRAVELLING EVERY DAY.

Published by ABC Books for the
AUSTRALIAN BROADCASTING CORPORATION
GPO Box 9994 Sydney NSW 2001

First published September 2005

National Library of Australia
Cataloguing-in-Publication entry
Weber, Jason.
  Train tough.
  ISBN 0 7333 1269 1.
  1. Physical education and training.
  I. Australian Broadcasting Corporation. II. Title.
613.7

Designed by vossdesign
Colour reproduction by Graphic Print Group, Adelaide, Australia
Printed and bound in Hong Kong, China by Quality Printing

The exercises and advice given in this book are in no way intended as a substitute for
medical advice and guidance. Consult your doctor before beginning this or any other
exercise program. The author and publisher take no responsibility for any injury that
may be caused as a result of applying the information in this book.

ACKNOWLEDGEMENTS

Thanks to my editor Jill Brown for her infinite wisdom and tireless patience in tolerating from me the birth of two children, the renovation of a house, endless procrastination and a Rugby World Cup to get this project home; to Jody Lee for her tolerance of my cryptic writing style; and the ABC for their commitment to the publishing of unknown Australian authors. This book looks great thanks to the ace photographer Hugh Hamilton, and the brilliant design skills of Ingo Voss.

Thanks to Phil Waugh and Lote Tuqiri for lending me their time in posing for the photos and to the hundreds of rugby players I have been involved with over the last ten years who have allowed me the opportunity to ply my trade with them.

Special thanks to Anna-Louise Bouvier, whose guidance and support both initiated this project and assisted greatly in seeing it through to the end, and for her magnificent conceptualisation of, understanding and teaching of human movement.

To Tony Boutagy for his generosity in allowing me to use his equipment in shooting the photographs and for taking part in a number of the shots.

Finally, and certainly not least of all, thanks to my family, most specifically my gorgeous wife Suse, for putting up with the endless discussions and ponderings about how 'the book' has been proceeding over the last three years.

CONTENTS

IN THE BEGINNING

TRAIN TOUGH BASICS

GOING FOR IT

PART 1
IN THE BEGINNING

A WORD (OR TWO) FROM JASON WEBER

1

This book focuses on one theme – high quality training for high quality results. Let's get started.

Train Tough is for anybody with aspirations for a better physical existence. It's for those of us athletes who might not (yet) be good enough to be courted by a major shoe company, but want to take physical training preparation seriously. Given that you're reading this, I'll assume I'm talking about you.

There are no gimmicks, no shortcuts and no requirement to buy products from my company. (Made easier by the fact I have no products or company.) There's nothing other than the tried-and-tested information that athletes put into use every day.

Add a serious injection of your enthusiasm and commitment and you've got a straightforward, no-nonsense recipe for success in whatever field of physical performance you choose to pursue.

So, what can you, the athlete – professional, amateur, recreational or otherwise – expect to gain from *Train Tough*?

Three things…

1 Focus
The knowledge to define the framework of your own training program.

2 Intensity
The ability to apply a single-minded approach to the preparation and execution of your training program.

3 Aggression
The motivation to access that raw, blood-boiling emotion that will help you achieve superior results.

Combining these components with some basic sports science, which is not in 'men in white coats' speak, will help you tap into your very own tailor-made training program.

TRAIN TOUGH

HOW DOES 'TRAIN TOUGH' REALLY WORK?

Part 1, *In the beginning*, sets the scene and makes it clear you have to establish a systematic game plan and pay attention to your attitude if you are going to succeed. Part 2, *Train tough basics*, gets into the nitty-gritty of sports science. Part 3, *Going for it*, contains all the training programs you'll ever need.

■ Chapter 4, 'Fundamentals of Training', gets you started and helps you to plan how to use your time effectively to get the most out of your body.

■ Chapter 5, 'Fitness', shows you how to implement a productive fitness program to overcome the training peaks and troughs. Find out how fit you are and discover what makes the human engine tick over. If you know how things work, you know how to fine-tune them.

■ Chapter 6, 'Force', explains the basic theory of strength training. With this knowledge you can build your muscle power to push your training to the next level.

■ Chapter 7, 'Nuts and Bolts', puts the theory into practice. It demonstrates the seven fundamental lifts you need to get the best results in the least amount of time, plus all the other exercises that are featured in the various programs.

■ Chapter 8, 'Foundation Training', explains the importance of building a rock-solid base by working on the core muscles around the spine. It blows the washboard stomach theory out of the water.

■ Chapter 9, 'Fusion Training', describes circuit training that combines strength training and body conditioning in a single session – two for the price of one!

■ Chapter 10, 'Flexibility', helps you to get over your fear of stretching. This is one of the most important, yet most neglected, aspects of fitness programs. It reduces injury and increases training skill level, not to mention prolonging your sporting life.

■ The training programs are the big, chunky stuff. There is something for everyone from the beginner to the more advanced athlete. They range from 'Getting Out of the Blocks' to the 'Sealed Section' (extreme training for fanatics) to help you get fitter, stronger, faster.

Before you leap into a training program, have a read through Parts 1 and 2. Familiarising yourself with the science is the best way to understand why you do a particular exercise and what effect it has on your body.

And a final pearl (or two) of wisdom from me…

I'm no millionaire tycoon or stockbroking whiz, but I understand there's one basic tenet of business that applies across the board: 'You've got to spend money to make money.' Apply this to the world of physical performance and it translates to: 'You've got to spill some blood to get results!' But given we humans are limited to the amount of blood we can lose, it's critical that we're *smart* about how we execute our plan.

Very simply, the theme running through *Train Tough* is to train hard – really hard – for specified periods, not hours or days on end. I want to empower you and motivate you to:

FORMULATE AN INFORMED AND SMART PLAN

GIVE IT EVERYTHING YOU'VE GOT

TRAIN TOUGH AND ENJOY THE RIDE!

PS
ALL THE ABBREVIATIONS USED THROUGHOUT ARE LISTED ON P 216

ATTITUDE IS
2 EVERYTHING!

Train Tough is for the recreational athlete. The person who's out there in the park or the gym, trying their best, knowing there's something better but not knowing how to find it. This is most definitely for the person who wants to 'have a big go'!

A recreational athlete is anyone who:

- wants to do more than just sit on a stationary bike for 30 min or routinely churn out 3 x 10 on the latest 'three easy payments' strength gismo

- likes to challenge themselves in a variety of physical pursuits

- competes for fun in club competitions in any sport, be it triathalon, track & field, surfing, martial arts, rugby, whatever

- doesn't like to be bound by the restrictions of a gym

- wants to find out just how far they can go!

The recreational athlete is someone who's a regular trainer looking for something different. _Train Tough_ is a method of training that isn't time-consuming yet delivers the type of training that is on a par with the training of a competitive athlete (more on that later). This training method is stimulating, varied and definitely challenging. It will push you to your limits, if you're big enough to take it on. The principles of training that competitive athletes apply to their sessions are just as applicable to the recreational athlete.

The major differences are that competitive athletes have:

- a coach to guide them

- a competition schedule to keep them focused.

In place of these things the recreational athlete needs to become self-sufficient. He needs to be able to put together a plan to effectively and realistically move forward. There is no easy way to do this. It takes a little time, dedication and focus, but in the long run it's time well spent and will pay dividends for your strength and fitness.

The first step toward success in any training program is having your head in the right place. That doesn't mean putting blinkers on to block out the rest of the world or burying your head in a bucket of sand and training like a psycho (although this certainly will achieve results). What it does mean is that you must be aware of three things:

1 What you are doing in your training
- how many times per week
- what type of program
- exercise choice — what sort of exercise you do and why you do it
- exercise technique — being aware of correct versus incorrect technique

2 Why you are doing the things you do
- understanding the mechanics of what you are doing and how it relates to your goals
- enjoying what you are doing or exercising for purely practical reasons

3 When you are going to do it
- commitment of your time
- commitment to a place to train

Asking yourself these questions will help you identify what you are doing with your training, and give you a realistic and brutally honest picture of what you *think* you are doing and what you are *actually* doing. It's all about taking and keeping control over the direction of your program. If you have control over the direction then you have control over the outcome. And achieving your desired outcome is what it's all about.

WHAT IS THE DIFFERENCE BETWEEN THE TRAINING PROGRAMS OF COMPETITIVE ATHLETES AND THE SLIPSHOD ACTIVITIES OF MANY RECREATIONAL ATHLETES?

DIRECTION
PRECISION
VARIETY

Direction

This is the single most important feature of the training program. If you lack direction you lack a meaningful purpose for training. Direction in your training allows you see the way forward on a session-to-session basis. Every day when you go to training you should be able to see in your mind's eye the value in the session you are doing. If you're only training for training's sake then you will struggle to achieve results. Worse still, if you're training because of a financial commitment to a gym or through guilt because of what you ate on the weekend you're heading down a desperate path that is never trodden by successful athletes.

DIRECTION is based on establishing a challenging yet achievable set of goals and going after them with a balanced and progressive program.

TRAIN TOUGH

Precision

This refers to the planning and execution of training. While competitive athletes and their coaches spend hours devising training regimes, the recreational athlete doesn't need to go this far. However, you have to commit some time to getting a few program parameters down on paper. *Write down your training goals and programming;* it's the only way to ensure your training moves onward and upward. Ad-hoc training where you just lob up and do what you feel like leads to a serious dead-end. Every gym in the world has examples of people who tend to:

- drift between exercises or machines they know (bench press and bicep curls tend to be the favourite of most males)

- stay on one piece of equipment for the entire session

- do nothing but socialise.

Doing any of the above is no way to achieve anything. Why waste the time? A small degree of planning in the initial stages of a program will boost your training ten-fold down the track.

REMEMBER:
PLAN THE WORK, WORK THE PLAN

Precision in the execution of training is a crucial part of success. Every session needs to be executed according to your plan, and done in an aggressive and controlled manner. There is no value in training like a zombie. To achieve results training needs to be conducted *aggressively and with purpose.* Apathy strikes everybody at some point, even the strongest athlete. This state of mind needs to be overridden by the desire to achieve the goals that you've set for yourself. The road map to help you to maintain discipline and focus is your training program. Another good solution for shaky motivation is training with a really focused individual – especially when you can see the results they're getting. Competition is a great motivator.

A single-minded focus aimed at getting the most out of yourself every time you train will help you to apply the effort required to achieve your goals.

For example, if your target is to run at 75–85 per cent of maximum heart rate (MHR) you need to run within that. Going off your nut and bolting around at 95 per cent MHR won't help you achieve your goals. Similarly, if the work-set of a strength program requires you to complete 6 reps at 150 kg in the squat, loading the bar with 180 kg will change the reps you're able to complete thereby changing the nature of the work-set away from your targeted zone.

Variety

The beauty of working from a structured program is that you can see precisely where you have been. With this knowledge under your belt it's a really simple matter to inject changes into your program so as to continually challenge your body and provide the stimulus for adaptation and the achievement of greater physical performance. Variety is the lifeblood of any training program, particularly as you become more experienced. The ability to introduce variety comes from a little bit of knowledge about what works and what's possible.

Remember though that no matter how much success you've had on a program, that success will diminish over time if the program is not changed. Herein lies the cause of most people's inability to produce results from exercise programs. Everybody, at some point, finds a 'favourite' program that works for them. Most people then seem to think that if they keep doing it forever they'll continue to improve. Not the case. Even the best program in the world from the best coach in the world needs to be changed regularly. The frequency with which you implement changes in your program is based on:

- How long you've been training. More experienced athletes need to change more often (maximum of 4-week cycles).

- The nature of the program. High intensity programs need to be altered every 2 – 3 weeks.

HOW TO AVOID THE FAILURE TRAP

Having spent the last 17 years in and around a variety of training venues I have come to understand that there are several general reasons why people fail to achieve their goals.

Set realistic goals

People who go to the gym with lofty expectations of being absolutely massive and ripped are more often than not kidding themselves. The time and commitment required to achieve extreme levels of response are beyond most people. Goals need to be set at a realistic level so that they're *obtainable*. Nobody ever made a donkey move by putting a carrot a mile in front of him.

The carrot is dangled just in front of the donkey so he thinks he can get it. Your lesson? If you set good, achievable goals you'll achieve good results. (Another is that it sucks to be a donkey.)

It's time for commitment

This comes down to that excellent quote:

> **'DON'T JUST TALK THE TALK; WALK THE WALK'.**

It's no good spouting off to friends and family that you're starting on a new training regime. Training should remain a resolute and personal pursuit. Rather than putting the cart before the horse and telling all and sundry about how much work you're going to do, let people remark on how much you've changed after they haven't seen you for a while. Let goal setting be about what you are trying to achieve remain internalised to help maintain your rock-solid focus.

> **THE BEST SESSION YOU EVER DO IS THE ONE NOBODY IS WATCHING.**

Translation: if you can go out and complete a challenging session to the letter of your program, by yourself, with nobody watching, no cheer squad, then you'll have the resolve, tenacity and commitment to get the job done.

Consistency goes a long way

Good results are achieved by consistent hard work – nothing more complicated than that. Most of the adaptations the body makes in response to training happen over a long period of time. These adaptations become stronger the longer you've been training, so it pays to remain consistent. By applying a systematic approach to consistent hard work you'll increase the efficiency of your training and reap the rewards of great results.

TRAIN TOUGH

Say no to low intensity training

Many people get caught up in the pattern of training at low intensity. This applies to both strength and fitness training. Bottom line: you can only lift 3 x 8 reps on 4 exercises or do 3 x 10 minutes on the bike, treadmill and stepper for so long before it becomes totally useless. Training *intensity* is the key variable to manipulate in order to achieve success.

The need to increase training loads and progress towards maximal loading is based on the theory that physical loads that are most capable of significantly disrupting homeostasis [your body's resting, 'normal' state], elicit the greatest training effect.

Dr Mel Siff, PhD (RSA), Dept. Biomechanical Engineering, Wits University, South Africa

BE WARNED: don't treat intensity lightly – it will bite you on the arse if used incorrectly.

TRAIN HA

TRAIN CO

TRAIN SM

REMEMBER:
THE WAY IN WHICH
YOU APPROACH YOUR TRAINING,
BOTH IN PLANNING AND EXECUTION,
IS THE KEY TO SUCCESS. UTILISING
AN AGGRESSIVE RESOLVE TO
ORGANISE YOUR SESSIONS AND
THEN EXECUTING THEM CORRECTLY
IS THE FOUNDATION ON
WHICH ALL RESULTS ARE BUILT.

ISTENTLY
T

EFFECTIVE
3 GOAL SETTING

Goal setting is a term thrown about by everybody from school counsellors to big-mouthed motivation and life coach speakers. Unfortunately it's the latter who contribute to this term being misinterpreted as something only self-important, insecure yuppies need worry about.

In fact the opposite is true. Goal setting is a task that coaches and athletes in all forms of elite sport take very seriously. The setting of appropriate and *achievable* goals allows the athlete to see the steps that need to be taken to get to the end result, the desired performance. Not understanding the power of effective goal setting means that a lot of people don't have an end point in mind when they take up an exercise program.

IF YOU DON'T KNOW WHERE YOU ARE GOING, HOW WILL YOU KNOW WHICH ROAD TO TAKE?

Goal setting can be as detailed or as simple as you like. It needn't be an involved process generating extra time and work. You must, however, commit your goals to paper. Writing down a goal shows your commitment to achieve a desired outcome. Just having a random thought in your head that you hang onto as your ultimate goal only leads to one thing: totally aimless training.

NO GOAL = NO FOCUS, which means inappropriate or ineffectual training. Why waste the time?

Even the downside of writing down goals is good. What's the worst that can happen? You don't achieve it! Well, that's not the end of the world. In fact, failing to achieve a goal after pursuing a particular course of action gives you the cold, hard facts that allow you to assess if:

1 The program was inappropriate.

2 The program was not completed with sufficient dedication.

3 The goal was inappropriate.

One or more of these three reasons is always present in a failed program. Realising where you've made a mistake allows you to re-assess your goals and move forward.

KEYS FOR SETTING GOOD GOALS

MAKE GOALS ACHIEVABLE AND REALISTIC

They need to be within reach. Good goals have a series of small steps in the same way you take the stairs step- by- step. 'You can't take the escalator to success; you can only take the stairs.'

MAKE GOALS PERFORMANCE–ORIENTATED NOT OUTCOME–ORIENTATED

Performance goals are defined by achieving an objective target, for example: 'Run 5 km under 20 min' or 'Complete 20 chin-ups'. Outcome-orientated goals, like 'Look fitter', are subjective and don't provide a specific finish line. Discerning whether an outcome-orientated goal has been achieved is based on interpretation; you can lie to yourself about having achieved it. Worse still, you can change the goal in your mind to accompany what you've achieved. Impress the guy in the mirror … don't bullshit him.

GIVE EACH GOAL A TIMEFRAME FOR RE-ASSESSMENT

Each goal must have a timeframe attached to it. For a goal to be effective it can't just hang out in the wind. Your goals are the framework around which the rest of your program is built and must be founded on a solid platform – dates. Having a date of re-assessment for each goal gives you a point to aim for.

The hardest thing about setting goals is knowing where to start. If you don't have a specific performance goal in mind from the outset you need to start very simply. Write down a couple of things you want to get out of your training program in one column and next to this column write down ways you think you can achieve this. Also write down realistic timeframes for achieving your goals. The next step is to arm yourself with the fundamental principles of training tough.

PART 2
TRAIN TOUGH BASICS

FUNDAMENTALS
4 OF TRAINING

The ability to improve physical performance is based on the natural adaptive processes of the human body. These processes have allowed us to grow both physically and intellectually to the point where we dominate our surroundings.

Physiological changes are based on our ability to maintain homeostasis – balance – within the body. In effect, the human body works within a fairly small tolerance range with regard to external stresses. These include:

- weather conditions (heat, cold, etc)

- emotional stress

- physical load (work, training, etc).

The human body doesn't like to be moved away from its normal (homeostatic) operating level too much. Therefore when confronted with a stress it will endeavour to maintain its current operating level. For example:

- Our body temperature averages about 38°C. If you go out and stand in a snow storm your body will lose heat. In order to retain the normal operating temperature, the body will begin the autonomic nervous system function of shivering. Shivering produces extra heat which maintains the temperature of the body.

- Digging a hole on a 40°C day will increase your body heat quite significantly. In response, your body employs the sweat mechanism to keep cool.

These are both automatic responses to stimuli, but the same type of mechanisms allow the human body to improve its athletic performance. A couple of examples:

1   Going for a run demands higher levels of oxygen be delivered to the working muscles. This means that the heart must beat more frequently to supply blood loaded with oxygen. However, there is a limit to how fast your heart can beat, which in turn limits the amount of blood that can be supplied.

With sufficient stimulus or exercise stress from regular runs, bike rides, rowing (or any other type of aerobic activity), the body actually *adapts* by increasing the size of the left ventricle in the heart (the chamber that propels blood through the body). How good is that? This change combined with an elevated heartbeat rate allows increased cardiac output, which means more blood gets pumped around the body.

2 Lifting the heaviest weight you can requires the recruitment (use of) the strongest fibres found in the muscles. In an untrained person these fibres are recruited in disorganised patterns that severely limit the production of maximal strength. Over a period of time, after being exposed to a significant training stimulus (like, say, lifting lots of heavy things), the body improves the muscle firing rate and the pattern of synchronisation of the required muscle fibres, thereby increasing the load that may be lifted. Amazing, huh?

There's one catch: the processes of adaptation that improve physical performance tend to work over a long period of time and require frequent and regular application of stimulus to achieve significant changes. Remember, the body wants to remain balanced despite the external stresses. If the training stimulus is stopped then the impetus for the body to remain at a high level of performance is reduced and performance will be reduced. This is where the training principle of *consistency* comes in.

Each system of the body that contributes to physical performance has its individual form of adaptation.

In general there are three types of adaptation:

1 **Biochemical (B).** Biochemical adaptations refer to the increase in activity of chemical processes within the body that contribute to improved performance, eg. increase in level of muscle enzyme PFK (phosphofructokinase) via specific training contributes to enhanced generation of energy via anaerobic pathways.

2 **Structural (S).** As a result of appropriate training stimulus the body may adapt its physical structure by way of increased laying down of proteins, eg. strength training contributes to increases in muscle size (hypertrophy) as a function of minute damage to muscle tissue followed by subsequent repair.

3 **Neurological (N).** The application of training stimulus in effect teaches the central nervous system how to communicate more efficiently with muscle tissues. This happens in a number of ways with the two most prevalent mechanisms being the increased rate of firing of muscle fibres and the improved coordination of activation of muscle units (synchronisation).

Structural and neurological changes tend to occur over a longer period of time and stay in place much longer. In most cases these are the physical elements of performance referred to as 'base training' (you may have heard the term 'aerobic base'). These training adaptations also tend to build up over time and are referred to as 'chronic' adaptations. Chronic adaptations form the foundation from which all superior performance is built.

Traditionally Eastern Bloc training systems have been largely based on huge amounts of general physical preparation (GPP). The level of GPP an athlete has 'under his belt' inevitably determines the degree to which he can sustain the more advanced levels of training.

To draw on one of the most overused analogies in training, GPP represents ongoing financial contributions to an investment fund. If you start out with a little, it will grow over time without much more attention than interest rates (standard training). However if you top it up regularly with extra base funds (GPP) the effect of the interest rates (standard training) will be much greater and will eventually yield superior

TRAIN TOUGH

GENRE	TYPE OF TRAINING	PHYSIOLOGICAL RESPONSE
Strength	HYPERTROPHY	Increased size of muscle fibres (S)
Strength	MAXIMUM STRENGTH	Increased muscle unit synchronisation (N)
Fitness	AEROBIC	Increase in cardiac output (left ventricle volume) (S)
		Increase in peripheral vascularity (more blood supply) (S)
		Increase in mitochondrial density (engine of cell that uses O_2) (S)
Fitness	ANAEROBIC	Increase in the enzymes that produce energy anaerobically (creatine kinase, phosphofructokinase, saythatwithagobfullofmarbles, etc) (B)
		Increase in acidic buffer capacity (ability to run harder, longer) (B)

performance. The effect of a solid base level of training, and continually adding to it over time, means that, while results are hard to achieve initially, these adaptations are slower to degrade over time.

Improvements in the biochemical strength of a physiological system often occur more quickly but are also quicker to reduce in potency. Athletic programmers spend a lot of time developing accurate planning techniques allowing this type of adaptation to be maximised and maintained. The human body will adapt depending on the nature of the external stress applied. Herein lies the true secret of developing your own effective training program. 'Adapt or die' is a law of Nature to which we are still, despite technology, subject to. So, stress your body with a stimulus and it will adapt and improve.

The ability to optimise individual adaptation is governed by:
- the prescribed training load (what's in your program)
- the motivation of the individual (how much you want it).

Therefore, the only thing between a motivated individual and the achievement of optimal performance is an accurate and efficient training program. Sounds too simple to be true…

The *limit* of *achievable* adaptation is determined by the inherent capabilities of the individual: their genetic make-up. The cruel truth is that some individuals adapt better than others, they move further forward physically, they're able to achieve more. There are scientific methods and 'experienced eye' techniques which can give an indication of your physiological potential. While ultimately nobody can give you a definitive answer, we do know that few people are operating anywhere near their best.

Chances are you aren't. Hopefully you will see this as a challenge that you're ready to take on with efficient training programs which take advantage of your body's natural adaptive ability, and by applying a measured dose of physical work then allowing recovery to enhance the process.

THE STRESS RECOVERY CYCLE

The key to an effective program is to fully understand the adaptive process described above. Research shows that even in recreational athletes of 80-years-plus, significant physical gains can be achieved through the correct application of the stress recovery cycle. Theoretically, this defines the time needed to allow the body to adapt to a training stimulus.

TRAIN TOUGH

The cycle goes like this:

■ training, which places a stress stimulus on the body

■ a degree of damage occurs to the body depending on the magnitude and intensity of the stimuli

■ after an appropriate recovery period (length determined by the nature of the stimulus) the body repairs itself to a level *beyond* where it started.

Managing the stress recovery cycle is the basis of good program design. Your training program needs to take into account several key points:

■ Your age
  • An older individual will adapt slower than a younger one.

■ Your training experience
  • A more experienced trainer will adapt quicker than a less experienced one.

■ Your desired outcome
  • The larger the goal, the more time required.

■ The types of training modes (running, swimming, XTR, etc) available
  • Available facilities may dictate program. Are you a gym member? Is there a park nearby?

■ Your level of motivation
  • 'You can lead a horse to water, but you can't make it drink.' A motivated individual will always succeed more than an unmotivated one.

The key to managing the stress recovery cycle is twofold:

1 **Listen to your body:** from session to session you should feel 'ready' to train again. If you are still sore or more fatigued than normal, postponing a session 12–24 hrs will generally allow you to perform better at the subsequent session and therefore gain more from your training. This is generally considered the art of programming training. In elite sport there are numerous convoluted methods of assessing an athlete's preparedness to train; however, for the man on the street, learning to listen to your body is the most effective way of assessing your readiness to train.

2 **Be honest:** this guideline is the antithesis of the previous one. DON'T BE A WIMP AND COP OUT OF TRAINING. This is truly a balancing act. There are times, particularly after a day at work, when you don't feel like training, but in fact it is absolutely the best thing for you to do. This is the time to *truthfully* take stock of the state of your body, and if everything checks out OK, then 'roll up your sleeves' and get into it. Taking the easy path when you simply don't feel like training is a sure way to achieve absolutely nothing.

PROGRESSIVE OVERLOAD

As you move forward in your training life, you will quickly find out that a single training session does not continue to have the same results over a long period of time. The need to advance the training stimulus is described by the principle of *progressive overload*.

In a nutshell, progressive overload simply means training harder over time. Well, increasing intensity is a better term. If you do the same session twice in a row with no break it will definitely make things a whole lot harder but won't be really beneficial. You will feel like you are training tough but the physical reality and the results will tell a completely different story. The secret to effective training is *intensity*. Progressively overloading intensity (adding more weight, running faster, speeding up on the treadmill, and so on) is far more efficient at getting the adaptive changes happening than just increasing volume (that is, doing more reps at a comfortable level).

All training performance is tied to the law of diminishing returns. In the early stages of a training program, particularly if you're inexperienced, your body will adapt effectively in a short period of time. However, as time goes on with the same program, the body adapts less and less, to the point that adaptation stops progressing. The same law of diminishing returns also applies to experienced trainers. As they get closer and closer to achieving their optimal performance, more time must be invested, but the gains are small. This is where progressive overload comes into its own as it ramps up your training and pushes your body to adapt to something new, so the improvement kicks in again.

It's of tremendous importance that beginners make a note of the *rate* of improvement that can be gained early in a training program. While it may be difficult to get started and the ego of certain males may take a battering initially, the gains a beginner can make are fantastic and should be used as a motivational tool. Make the most of it while it lasts!

DETRAINING

Detraining is an effect with which too many people are familiar without even knowing it. It happens when a performance variable (strength, fitness, and so on) is not provided with sufficient stimulus to improve. This occurs for two reasons:

1 Training stops, and no stimulus is provided.

2 Training continues at the same level (of intensity and volume), the body adapts initially and then as the stimulus fails to change, performance begins to drop.

PRACTICAL TIPS FOR AVOIDING DETRAINING

Add one 'change up' session to your program every 2 weeks, for example:

STRENGTH TRAINING: If you are lifting mostly lower reps (2–6) in your current program add in a session using 8–12 reps.

FITNESS TRAINING: If you are doing mostly longer work (5–10 min efforts) add in a session using 2–3 min at a slightly higher intensity.

For experienced lifters change your key lifts every 2–3 weeks (4–5 weeks for less experienced).

Change the focus of your program every 4–5 weeks (more experienced athletes may need to change every 3–4 weeks), for example:

Strength: Week 1–4
Hypertrophy (5–6 exercises, 3–4 sets, 8–12 reps),
Week 5–8
Strength (3–4 exercises, 3–6 sets, 4–6 reps).

Fitness: Week 1–4
Aerobic Base (3–4 efforts approx. 10min HR Zone 2, see p 36)
Week 5–8
Aerobic Power (5 efforts approx. 6min HR Zone 3, see p 36).

AND THE POINT OF ALL THIS – APPLY VARIETY TO YOUR TRAINING

RATE OF RECOVERY/REGENERATION

Every time you train you generate an element of fatigue which causes your body to lapse into a period of reduced functional capacity. (That's boffin-speak for: 'You get tired and can't run as far or lift as much.') In time the system that's been trained (your fitness, strength, and so on) regenerates to an *improved* functional capacity, thereby improving performance.

The rate of recovery from a single training session will determine the appropriate time to complete the next training session. If two or more demanding sessions are completed in succession then recovery will be compromised. For example:

■ Squatting heavy 3 days in a row.

■ Running a hard 4 km interval session 3 days in a row.

It's not advisable to pursue this form of loading as it rarely results in improved performance and puts you at risk of overuse injury. In many cases this is the pattern of the 'binge' trainer, the guy who goes really hard for a short period until he finds himself so stuffed that training is no longer enjoyable. (Yes, it's supposed to be enjoyable.) The rate of recovery will also be affected by the following factors:

■ Older people require more time to recover than younger people.

■ More experienced trainers will recover faster than less experienced. (See, it pays to train regularly.)

TRAIN TOUGH

- Higher fitness levels in a particular training mode will enhance recovery. (Ditto on the training regularly.)

- The fitter you are the faster you will recover.

- Training in an unfamiliar environment may slow recovery.

- High levels of emotional stress will slow recovery.

Recovery training: What the...?

As mentioned earlier, many superior athletes invest a lot of time in GPP (general physical preparation). You'll recall this type of training continually improves the athlete's 'training base'. As luck would have it, this is one occasion when it is possible to knock over two training aims in one session. Following a particularly hard session, one of the best modalities to enhance recovery from that session is to lightly train again in that mode.

For example:
- Following a hard squatting session (4–6 sets, 2–6 reps building to maximum effort), the next day's session may be comprised of light step ups, walking lunges and glute ham raises.

The idea of the 'recovery session' is not to apply a training stimulus that will cause greater fatigue, but rather one that will allow the joints used to regain their range of motion (reduce stiffness experienced after a hard session). There's also the added benefit of having added a further light training stimulus.

Now that you've taken all of the technical stuff into account, it's time to start planning your training schedule. Yep, I said planning.

TAKING RECOVERY TO THE EXTREME

One of Australia's rising stars of international rugby has been known to feel so 'aggressive' during recovery sessions that he has achieved PB's in bench press (>150 kg) the day after a game. By listening to his body he knows when to 'have a go', even if the timing seems odd by conventional standards.

EVERYONE, AND I'M ALSO TALKING TO THOSE MADMEN AMONG YOU, SHOULD ALLOW A MINIMUM OF ONE DAY OFF PER WEEK.

Guidelines for setting a weekly training plan, taking into account the recovery/regeneration factor

■ Sessions that require near maximum effort shouldn't be planned for the same (that is, running, squats, etc) more than twice a week. This simply means that if you plan to run a time trial or lift a maximum in squat, you should avoid doing the same activity at a similar level of intensity again in the same week.

■ Alternate training may be pursued while your recovery is taking place in another variable.

AN EXAMPLE

Monday: Weights
Tuesday: Running
Wednesday: Weights
Thursday: Running
Friday: Weights

Your lesson: Alternating training modes daily allows your body to recover from the previous day.

ANOTHER EXAMPLE

Monday: Hard interval sprints
Tuesday: Medium pace jog
Wednesday: Hard swim
Thursday: Medium pace jog
Friday: Hard interval sprints

Your lesson: Alternating between hard and easy days (that is, Monday anaerobic/Tuesday aerobic) allows recovery because different energy systems are being used. Changing modes on Wednesday (swim) allows recovery from the previous days' running.

TRAINING ORGANISATION

The systematic organisation of training was largely developed in Eastern European countries and given the term *periodisation*. Very simply, it's an organisational structure allowing you to plan the *development* of your physical performance. Periodisation can be an extended and complicated process at the elite end of the market (competitive athletes need to peak for competition, multi-peak for different competitions, maintain peaks through long seasons, etc) but the basic principles are easily applied to the recreational athlete.

There are 4 areas of your program that you need to establish:

1 WEEKLY
2 MONTHLY
3 QUARTERLY
4 YEARLY

And within those, a basic order of training elements must be adhered to.

Strength

1 Anatomical adaptation (your muscles adapt to stimuli)
2 Hypertrophy (your muscles grow)
3 Maximum strength (you become stronger…)
4 Power (…and faster)

Fitness

1 Aerobic base (using O_2 slowly)
2 Aerobic power (using O_2 quickly)
3 Threshold (the level at which your body switches gear from aerobic to anaerobic)
4 Lactic acid tolerance (how much anaerobic work you can sustain)

Each level lays the platform for the next. By improving at the lower level you give yourself a spring-board to launch into the next cycle. Each element must be addressed in the correct order. Attempting programs contrary to this structure is asking for trouble. The only thing that will be achieved by pursuing this path is injury.

REMEMBER: YOU'VE GOTTA TRAIN SMART TO TRAIN TOUGH.

FITNESS
5 MAXING YOUR ENERGY LEVELS

The first step towards getting your own productive fitness program up and running is understanding some of the basics of how the human engine works and using this information to get more out of your workout.

The body needs energy to power muscles and organs, and for many of you the terms 'aerobic' and 'anaerobic' might ring a bell. Fitness is generally broken down into two systems based on the relationship between oxygen and energy.

> **NOTE**
> 1 = Aerobic
>
> 2 = Anaerobic — alactic system
>   lactic acid system

1   *Aerobic energy metabolism* simply means that this energy system needs oxygen as part of its chemical process to function. Oxygen is taken in by the lungs (respiratory system) and supplied to the muscles by the heart and circulatory network (cardiovascular system). This produces low levels of power with no chemical by-products produced in the muscles (lactic acid is the primary by-product of energy metabolism that contributes to fatigue). It takes a while for this energy system to start functioning effectively, approximately 3–4 min, after which this becomes the main source of energy production.

2   The anaerobic energy system, by definition, is a form of energy metabolism that doesn't require oxygen in the production of energy for muscular contraction (but this doesn't necessarily mean you can stop breathing … read on).

The anaerobic energy system itself can be divided into two categories:

1   The alactic system breaks down chemicals within the muscle to produce energy. This is classically known as the 'fight or flight' energy supply as it activates rapidly, producing high power for a short time

ATP – WHAT THE HELL IS IT?
Science geeks know this as *adenosine triphosphate* which is a molecule that is often referred to as the currency of energy production. To provide energy for muscle contractions, ATP is broken down. The process of this molecular breakdown creates energy and it is this energy that causes the muscle to contract. This energy supply is, however, limited. But the good news is that once broken down, ATP can be reformed and you can use this to boost your training.

(approximately 0–10 sec) and is the primary source of energy for explosive duration events, such as picking up a weight, running or swimming short distances in fast, powerful bursts. This system doesn't last long in the energy stakes but it recovers quickly, only needing about 2–3 min to be back at full throttle capacity.

2   The lactic acid system kicks in as the alactic system begins to slow down and is capable of producing medium levels of power output for a maximum period of approximately 2–3 min (optomised at approximately 60 sec). The by-product of this system is lactic acid, which in sufficient amounts causes reduction in muscle power, poor coordination and nausea. This system is generally used when exercise intensity exceeds the capabilities of the aerobic system (for instance, when an 800 m runner is struggling down the final stretch). Recovery from this system is a lot slower, taking up to 45–60 min.

MAKING SENSE OF THE SCIENCE

While it's easy to compartmentalise different energy supplies, in practice they don't work the way they do on paper. The aerobic and the anaerobic systems are always working together. It is the intensity of effort which determines how much oxygen is available in the cells for your body to use. Energy supply exists based on the level of power produced and the time span of the exercise.

In theory, the alactic system is the fastest energy system and hence the most dominant during activities like running a 100 m sprint. The lactic acid system comes in second as the dominant energy supplier in sustained exercise, for example, a 400 m run. The aerobic systems come on line

last and this gives you the energy needed for even longer bouts of exercise. That said, when completing longer efforts, say a 3 km run (which is primarily an aerobic event), the lactic acid system allows you to pick your pace up beyond that which you can sustain aerobically (for example, overtaking a dawdling opponent or attacking the hills).

Overtaking or attacking hills while running is the perfect example of the effect of lactic acid. Running at a sustainable pace essentially means you are supplying energy primarily via aerobic mechanisms. By picking up the pace you are using more of the high-powered lactic acid system to produce the power required for increased speed. This comes at a price: lactic acid. The pick up in pace is only sustainable for a short period of time, then you must return to a pace at which the body can both supply energy for the activity via aerobic means, and also clear out the remnants of the lactic acid.

Too much science; let's go to some practical examples.

■   Surf boat racing is generally done over a course that takes around 6 min. Strictly speaking it's an aerobic event. However, because absolute maximum effort is used, there's a very significant anaerobic contribution (primarily from the lactic acid system) to the event. It becomes the dominant system from approximately 3 min onwards.

Energy supply rating:
aerobic 50 per cent, anaerobic 50 per cent

- A superior cross-country runner might complete a 5 km course in about 15 min. Again, this is technically an aerobic event but, because of the high speed required to win and the variable terrain, a high 'lactate tolerance' level is required to keep pushing the limits to make it to the finish line.

Energy supply rating:
aerobic 70 per cent, anaerobic 30 per cent

- An interval session comprised of 5 x 2 min sets on a rowing machine hitting greater than 650 m per set with 90 sec recovery between sets (hold onto to your balls, boys!). A 2 min work set is toward the end of the lactic acid system's domain, but each set will be propped up by the aerobic system. The fact that the recovery period is not long enough to allow complete recovery ensures this. To complete this you need a strong aerobic base.

Energy supply rating:
aerobic 40 per cent, anaerobic 60 per cent

The examples above illustrate that rarely are we operating simply on one energy system. At most times during exercise we use a combination of energy systems, depending, of course, on what it is we are doing. A simple way to conceptualise the whole energy metabolism thing is this: *speed comes at a price!* The faster you want to go, the more energy you are going to need to liberate (breakdown of ATP), and the faster you go the greater the production of waste (lactic acid), which when present in sufficient quantities will force you to slow down.

How the energy systems work in the real world

Both forms of the anaerobic system work whenever you move. Lactic acid is produced all the time! At low intensities of exercise (say, changing the channel with the remote) the rate of lactic acid removal matches its production. Therefore there's no accumulation of lactic acid and subsequently no nasty, painful side effects from its production. (Unless, of course, *Neighbours* comes on the telly.) However, as exercise intensity – and hence lactic acid production – increases, a point is reached at which lactic acid production exceeds the rate of removal; you get a lactic acid surplus and you'll experience the nasty side effects of intense training: pain, fatigue, nausea.

The good news is that you can train your body to:
1 delay the point at which lactic acid begins to accumulate

2 tolerate higher levels of lactic acid (or lactate tolerance)

3 increase the rate of clearance of lactic acid.

The point at which lactic acid production begins to exceed removal has been termed the anaerobic threshold (AT). In practice, it pays to conceptualise the existence of AT as a 'zone' rather than a single point. If you're training within the AT zone, lactic acid accumulation is becoming more pronounced and any increase in training intensity will cause your exercise duration to have a very finite timeframe (you will have to stop very soon because some heavy-duty fatigue is beginning to set in).

SPEED COMES AT A PRICE!

ANAEROBIC THRESHOLD

Throughout the 70's and 80's the scientific community turned itself inside out explaining, debating and theorising the concept of the AT. Theoretically, it defines the point at which the dominant energy system changes from aerobic to anaerobic. Now as interesting as this is (well, at least for us sports nerds), the most important point to grasp is that different energy systems are operating simultaneously all the time.

TRAIN TOUGH

INTENSE TRAINING

When you're looking to put together a program with the correct training *intensity*, these energy systems need to be understood in order to get the best out of your body.

EXERCISE CAN BE DEFINED BY:

VOLUME (how long, how far, how much)

INTENSITY (heart rate, speed, rate of lactic acid production)

FREQUENCY (how often)

Intensity is a key component in session planning. You need to understand that intensity doesn't mean how hard training is or feels, as this is quite often way off the mark and can lead to some common training mistakes.

- Training too hard may cause injury, excessive fatigue and loss of interest (due to being consistently flogged).

- Training too easy will not supply sufficient stimulus for the body to adapt and improve.

The easiest way to monitor intensity is by the heart rate (HR). The heart is the engine of the body. Quite simply it pumps oxygen-rich blood from the lungs to the working muscles then ships out all the waste products to the lungs, kidneys, and so on for disposal. Your body responds like a car: the more you push the accelerator, the more the engine revs. However, in the case of the human body, the engine's revs are monitored by beats per minute (bpm).

Working out your maximum heart rate (MHR)

As with any engine, the heart has an end point beyond which it cannot pass. Knowing, or at least taking an educated guess at, this number allows training sessions to be conducted at an intensity level suited to the individual.

Due to a number of predominantly genetic factors, MHR is specific to the individual. Exercise intensity cannot be arbitrarily attributed to a

WHY THIS PROCESS IS IMPORTANT

When I started working with the Australian Sevens Rugby team they had been completing some generic interval work using 175 bpm as their target HR. Some players mentioned that it was extremely hard to achieve the target HR, while another stated that he wasn't sure if he 'should be going so slow'. A quick field test indicated that there was significant difference between MHR in several players.

Player A: MHR = 181 bpm
Player B: MHR = 203 bpm

For Player A, a target HR of 175 bpm represents greater than 96 per cent of his MHR. This places him within a few per cent of his MHR, which is not a good place to be from the outset during a series of interval runs.

Player B's MHR of 203 bpm means he was running at 86 per cent of his MHR. His training load needed to be a little higher.

The lesson:
Training to a HR needs to be specific to the individual.

single HR. For example, a person whose heart has large ventricular volume will typically have a lower HR than someone with small ventricular volume, as the amount of blood that can be pumped every beat is larger. Other factors such as the nature of the cardiac tissue, the resistance against which the heart has to pump and fitness all contribute to individual MHR.

While pushing your heart to its limit may sound dangerous, the reality is that in a healthy individual taking your heart rate to maximum presents no risk to your health (other than the fact you have to do some very hard work).

However…

From a safety point of view, anybody over the age of 35 or with a family history of heart disease or abnormality should consult their doctor before embarking on a MHR discovery mission.

While it's considered safe for a healthy individual to take their HR to the max, it is not advisable to do this if you are starting out on a beginner's training program. Start off slow and safe; work on building your basic fitness level before attemping a MHR field test.

There are a number of methods that may be used to determine MHR. In order of accuracy they are:

- lab assessment

- field test

- age-based estimate.

Lab assessment

This is typically run on a treadmill at a specialist facility like a university with sport science or human movement programs. 'Stress' tests of this nature are generally combined with other measures of physiological performance such as maximum oxygen uptake (MVO_2) and lactate curves. This information can be analysed in a number of ways to provide detailed training information.

The test consists of a graded protocol where the speed of the treadmill gets faster and higher to the point at which the subject can no longer continue (known as 'volitional exhaustion', also known as 'rooted'). This type of test has a very small margin of error.

This type of assessment is suitable for:

- serious athletes (competitive or recreational)

- individuals over 35 years

- individuals with a family history of heart disease or abnormalities

- individuals who have never taken their HR to the maximum or are just beginning a training regimen.

TRAIN TOUGH

The field test of MHR
Equipment needed:
- ■ HR monitor (preferably recordable)

- ■ flat running surface (with a a long slight incline nearby)

STEP 1
Warm up for 15 min, building your heart rate up slowly to a point at which you are sweating steadily and your breathing rate is slightly above normal.

STEP 2
Run for about 6 min. Try to add 10 to15 bpm by increasing your running speed approximately every 90 sec. As you get close to the 6 minute mark you should be flying!

STEP 3
Then hang onto the 'crown jewels' and go flat out for as long as you can (you should last between 45 sec to 90 sec if you've judged it correctly).

STEP 4
When you feel like your lungs are busting and your heart's hammering, give it one final effort, keeping an eye on your HR every couple of seconds. It should be edging up! When you see it start to fall the test is over and, you guessed it, the highest number you saw is your MHR.

MANIAC TIP
A nice touch is to finish the last sprint on a long slow hill (low to moderate level incline). Don't try going up a steep hill as local muscle fatigue in the legs may stop you from hitting a MHR.

An important aspect of attempting a run of this type is attitude. You must *want* to push your body to the end of its ability. Don't even waste your time if you're just doing it because it 'says so in the book' or if it's some sort of macho stripe on your shoulder. It needs to be a maximum effort aimed solely at seeing how high you can get the watch to go.

Even though the final stage is technically described as being painful, it is absolutely empowering to push yourself to the end of your body's capability. (It is!) For most people the limit to superior physical performance is their mind. Toward the end of a physical task like this it feels very much like one of those cartoons in which a tiny angel is perched on your right shoulder and a little devil is on the left. The angel has a soothing voice that keeps telling you: 'It's OK. You don't have to do this. We can just go home and lie on the nice cosy couch and eat chips.' Meanwhile the little devil is yelling: 'Keep going you soft M*&^#R F$%&#R. Don't even think about stopping! You've got more in the tank! *give it everything!*' (Funny, I think I sound like that at work sometimes.) In this case you've got to listen to the devil. He's providing you with the aggression and drive you need to complete this session and get the desired result.

SOME MOTHERS DO HAVE 'EM

Not too many years ago my brother and I use to do a regular boxing session that achieved MHR all too frequently. Using focus mits and fast alternating strikes (L-R-L-R), we would complete 8 to 10 x 2 min sets wearing a HR monitor transmitter but no watch. The watch was left on Mum's outdoor table so that at no point during the set could we see what HR we were getting.

The aim of each set was to see who could get the highest HR (we both had the same MHR) and we weren't allowed to check it with the watch until the end of every set. One point was awarded to the winner of every set. The winner of the session was simply the guy with the most points. Being very competitive, as all good brothers are, we would both hit MHR after 1 to 2 sets. Plenty of blood, sweat and tears was spilt on those sessions I can assure you!

This session was the flashing light bulb that spawned the idea for FTS SKINS – see Chapter 9, 'Fusion Training'.

Age-based estimate of MHR

For anyone starting out on exercise program for the first time or someone who is unfit, this is the easiest method to use in order to get started. These equations are based on average heart rate maximums, which as mentioned earlier are not specific to individuals.

Simple equations explain everything:

Male MHR:
220 minus your age equals your MHR

Female MHR:
226 minus your age equals your MHR

It's important when using these equations to be aware that your MHR may be over-estimated. This means that when you calculate your training intensities they may be overestimated as well. This will manifest itself as target heart rates that might feel too difficult.

TRAIN TOUGH

WORKING OUT INDIVIDUAL TRAINING ZONES

Once you know your MHR, you can plan sessions that work your heart at various percentages of it. The general structure of the training zone system is outlined in the table below.

These five zones plus the recovery zone represent different levels of stress being placed on the body. Each has its own characteristics and limits.

Recovery (< 60 per cent MHR)

Recovery HR zone is used, as the name would suggest, after serious training as a way of allowing your body to recover back to its optimum operating level. Recovery sessions generally take place in a relaxed environment and may involve a swim (pool or beach), light bike ride or a walk. The key element behind the recovery training zone is that you don't generate any extra fatigue or waste products. The focus is on clearing waste and reinvigorating the fatigued athlete.

Zone 1 (60 per cent to 75 per cent MHR)

Aerobic base (AB)/Zone 1 training is used for base aerobic development and improvement of muscular endurance. Athletes training for events such as triathlons, marathons and other long distance events will spend most of their time in Zone 1. Many of the structural changes (increase in blood supply, increase in oxygen processing) that contribute to greater endurance happen in this training zone. Recreational athletes just getting started would be well advised to spend some time in Zone 1 as it helps to increase the rate of recovery during more intense training modes. This pace should be easy and sustainable, you should be able to carry on a conversation without getting out of breath.

Zone 2 (75 per cent to 85 per cent)

Aerobic power (AP)/Zone 2 training marks the beginning of more intense training and works to improve on many of the training benefits in Zone 1 while adding a little bit of speed. At this pace your breathing rate will increase but you should still be able to have a conversation without getting out of breath. This zone represents the limit of 'steady state' performance, meaning you should be able to sustain this pace at the same level for a considerable amount of time.

HEART RATE ZONE	TRAINING RANGE	TRAINING GOAL/USE
Recovery	< 60 per cent MHR	Recovery (R)
Zone 1	60 per cent – 75 per cent MHR	Aerobic base (AB)
Zone 2	75 per cent – 85 per cent MHR	Aerobic power (AP)
Zone 3	85 per cent – 90 per cent MHR	Anaerobic threshold (AT)
Zone 4	90 per cent – 95 per cent MHR HI	Lactic acid tolerance (LAT)
Zone 5	95 per cent – Maximum MHR Max	Maximum effort (MAX)

Training in Zones 1 and 2 improves the body's overall ability to tolerate work through greater efficiency of the aerobic metabolism and improved muscular conditioning.

Zone 3 (85 per cent to 90 per cent)

Anaerobic threshold (AT)/Zone 3 training is aimed at training the body in the grey zone that is the theoretical anaerobic threshold (AT). The body is beginning to work at a pace that can no longer be sustained predominantly by aerobic metabolism. As the anaerobic metabolism begins to become more dominant, lactic acid begins to accumulate and the comfort level of training decreases. This is a crucial training pace as it allows your body to become more accustomed to working in an *acidic* environment, that is starting to deal with the effects of lactic acid. Having a conversation in this zone of training should now be quite difficult.

Zone 3 training is considered a bridge between Zones 1–2 and Zones 4–5.

Zone 4 (90 per cent to 95 per cent)

Lactic acid tolerance/Zone 4 training is used for interval training for improving sprinting speed, lactic acid tolerance and recovery from repeated sprints. Interval training periods typically last from 1–4 min and if you follow the conversation test, it'll resemble panting gibberish.

Zone 5 (95 per cent to maximum)

Maximum effort (Max)/Zone 5 training is reserved for maximum effort interval series based on improving lactate power (the ability to produce maximal lactate levels is an indication of the power of the anaerobic system). Improving lactate power gives you the ability to apply

maximal sprints for a limited period of time, something that is of tremendous value in many sporting environments. Interval training periods generally range from 60 sec to 90 sec. Conversation is impossible, as your lungs should be screaming for oxygen.

Zones 4 to 5 training tends to be used only by individuals going for a high performance level. Followed correctly these training levels can add new dimension to the recreational athlete's program by pushing you to higher levels of training performance.

TRAIN TOUGH

THE BIG HEAVY STUFF: TRAINING EQUIPMENT

Once you get the **how** and **why** of your training program sorted out, you need to get a handle on the **what.** Training modes (the actual exercise you do) can be as simple or diverse as you care to make them. Remember, variety is a key element of a solid training program.

Fitness isn't just about pounding the pavement. There are generally two modes of training.

1 Locomotion modes: activities where the athlete provides the energy to propel the body forward; that is, running, riding a bike, paddling a kayak, swimming, and so on. These modes tend to be 'real world', activities which are for the most part harder (but far more enjoyable) than their cross training equivalents. In my humble opinion these modes of training tend to be extremely good for the soul. They get you outside, experiencing a bit of nature and propelling yourself forward under your own steam. Added to this you get the benefit of actually going somewhere as opposed to, say, a treadmill, which no matter how fast you run on will never let you go anywhere (a very biased opinion I know, but it's mine and I'm sticking to it).

2 Cross training (XTR) modes: activities where the athlete remains stationary and exerts energy against an external resistance; that is, treadmill running, orbit walkers, steppers, stationary bikes, rowing ergometers.

Based on the division of training modes detailed above, let's have a look at the pros and cons of some of the main elements of each mode of training.

EXERCISE	POSITIVES	NEGATIVES
Running (real world)	High energy expenditure. Outdoor activity (good for the soul). Very good social activity.	Ankles, hips and knees may suffer in the untrained or heavier individual.
Swimming (real world)	Body weight is 100 per cent supported, which means limited injury risk. Energy expenditure moderate to high based on experience. Ocean swimming is a fantastic pastime (if fish don't bother you).	Technique may limit the inexperienced swimmer's ability to expend energy (beginners tend to need to sprint just to stay afloat).
Bike (real world)	Medium–high energy expenditure.Outdoor activity (good for the soul).	Poor bike set-up can lead to sore 'bits and pieces' (get a good bike-mechanic). Stray dogs can cause the odd problem.
Treadmill running (XTR)	High energy expenditure. Reduction in stress on lower limbs due to force absorption by treadmill.	Speeds don't transfer well to normal running (because belt speed assists running speed).
Orbit walker with arm action (without question my preferred piece of XTR equipment)	High–very high energy expenditure (go hard – excellent piece of equipment!). Non-impact activity.	You'll probably 'smash' yourself! *(in the right person this is a good thing).*
Steppers	Medium–high energy expenditure. Machines with independent steps are by far the best!	Waste of time unless step height is approx. equal to the knee of the opposite leg (if you don't feel it in the glutes then you are stepping too short).
Stationary bike	Medium–high energy expenditure. Non-impact activity.	Bike options may restrict positioning – make sure seat is high enough (see a qualified coach). Can be a bit sad sitting in a gym!
Rowing ergometers	High–very high energy expenditure (go hard – excellent piece of equipment). Non-impact activity. Only for the strong!	Back may suffer with poor technique (see a qualified coach).

FORCE
6 THE WHAT, WHY AND HOW

Strength training is all about one thing, the development of force. Once you get that, you're on your way to maxing your strength and power.

Force is described in physics as:

F (FORCE) = M (MASS) X A (ACCELERATION)

Using variables associated with the two components of force, that is, mass and acceleration, we can manipulate the way in which force is developed in order to achieve a variety of results. For example, we can focus on the very slow development of force that will contribute to an increase in muscle size (hypertrophy) or conversely the rapid development of force that will contribute to the development of power and speed.

MUSCLE STRUCTURE
There are three types of muscle tissue in the body, but there's only one kind that you need be concerned with here – skeletal muscle tissue.

This means the muscles that attach to and move your skeleton. The other types of muscle are cardiac (heart muscle) and 'smooth' muscle (internal organs).

Skeletal muscle tissue is usually found in bundles forming the different shapes and sizes of muscle groups that exist throughout the body (obviously some are bigger than others). Muscles are connected to your bones by tendons and they act voluntarily, which means you can use your brain to move 'em.

Down the track this becomes an important element to understand, as the further you progress in strength training the more training is focused on getting the neuromuscular system (brain, nerves and muscles) working in a more efficient manner rather than simply making the muscle itself bigger.

For those who wagged Human Biology 101, muscles and bones (the skeletal system) work together in a system of levers. One end of the muscle stays still while the whole muscle contracts and shortens, moving the other end of the muscle across a joint, which flexes the joint and causes the limb to move. There are a number of variations on this model throughout the vast array of joints in the body but this is the nuts and bolts of how we move.

Muscle fibre is divided into three different types:

1 **Slow twitch (ST) or Type I is a slow contracting muscle.**

   - It produces a limited amount of power but is resistant to fatigue.

   - It is efficient at maintaining posture and sustaining prolonged, low-intensity activity, such as jogging and most tasks of human movement.

   - This muscle is responsible for performance in primarily aerobic-based exercises and activities.

2 **Intermediate, fast twitch(a), (FT(a) or Type II(a)) is a fast contracting muscle.**

   - It produces a medium amount of power and is moderately resistant to fatigue.

   - It is suited to fast, repetitive, medium-intensity movement. Depending on the training history of the individual these fibres may function efficiently at either end of the power/endurance spectrum.

   - Given their adaptability these fibres can contribute to many elements of performance, from medium to high range strength performance (approximately 4–12 reps) to busting over hills in a 3 km run.

3 **Fast twitch(b), (FT(b) or Type II(b)) is a fast contracting muscle.**

   - It produces high levels of power with a rapid rate of fatigue.

   - It is suited to high power production; only recruited when very rapid or intense activity is required, such as maximum low range (1–3 reps) strength lifts or sprinting.

> Fast twitch fibres constitute what are known as 'high threshold motor units', which means that they require a very high degree of stimulation from the central nervous system to be activated. These motor units are not utilised on a day-to-day basis unless very intense training methods are instituted, for example, maximum sprinting, heavy lifting (1–3 reps) or maximum isometric contractions.

It's important to remember – as was pointed out to me by a biochemist friend – that muscle fibres aren't all one or the other of the above-mentioned classifications. They tend to blend between classifications, existing on a fibre 'continuum' (check out the diagram below) based on varying levels of power production and fatigability.

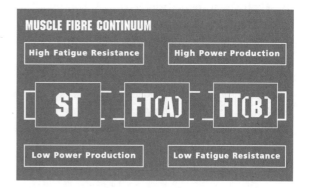

TRAIN TOUGH

Muscles are made up of varying numbers of cells with varying properties. The nature of an individual's cell content is largely determined by genetics (you can't pick your parents). Recent research suggests that the possibility exists for some movement toward either end of the power or fatigue-resistance spectrum based on chronic (long term) levels of training. This supports the theory that consistent training over a long period of time does bear fruit. So those of you who are 'binge' trainers, keep this in mind every time you give up for a few weeks; you're more than likely just letting yourself slip back to your physiological starting point.

WHY DOES STRENGTH TRAINING WORK?

Strength training is based on two key points:

1 Mechanical stress

2 Time under tension

Mechanical stress

This refers to the absolute weight that is being lifted. Muscle tissue will respond faster to a set of repetitions completed with a greater weight than a lighter one. The effect of mechanical stress on the muscle is by far the greatest stimulus for muscle tissue to hypertrophy (grow). So, if you've spent the last 12 months punching out 10–12 reps for 30 sets (total session, all exercises) and are wondering why you aren't growing, one reason may be that you simply aren't providing enough stimulus to the muscle – you've got to constantly challenge your muscles to improve otherwise they simply sit back and think they are good enough. The beauty of training is that as long as the muscle is challenged (trained) in the correct environment (that is, with good recovery, food, and so on) it must respond by improving, it has no choice.

Time under tension

This refers to the amount of time a muscle is subjected to external resistance, how long you're holding up the weight or how long a set takes to complete. Up to a maximum of approximately 60 sec and the muscle will be stimulated to grow in the presence of sufficient mechanical stress. Muscles thrive on mechanical stress.

So, the efficient development of muscular size and strength is a balancing act between the size of the weight and the amount of time it takes you to lift it. If you can manage these two variables the results will follow. It's a given.

HOW TO STRENGTH TRAIN EFFICIENTLY

Now you've mastered the 'what' and the 'why', let's move on to the 'how', the practical perspiring stuff.

BEFORE YOU START

Everybody has travelled at some point and had to refer to a map. The only really effective way to use one is to first establish where exactly (or as close as you can figure) you are on the map. The same applies if you are serious about your strength training. You need to know where you are at before you start trying to plot your course. By establishing your one repetition maximum (1RM), either by estimation or actually lifting a 1RM, you have a good idea of what your current strength levels are. This allows you to set a program to go forward. Refer back to your 1RM as both a guide for training and also a marker to allow you to assess your progress.

WORKING OUT 1RM

Getting injured at the gym is *stupid* and *avoidable*. Don't risk lifting a 1RM if you are not experienced and you don't have experienced people around you. I can't stress that enough.

Estimating a 1RM may be done in a number of ways using a multitude of different formulas. The benefit of using the following one is that it is conservative and therefore will allow you to train within your current capacity and push on as you gain confidence, rather than starting you at a generous estimate and having you work to your limit from the outset.

Guidelines for using 1RM

■ An actual 1RM attempt should be restricted to experienced lifters.

■ *Never* compromise technique in order to achieve a higher weight.

■ Always use spotters.

■ Any exercise may be used but in general stick to the 'big ones' such as squat, deadlift, bench press.

REPS – HOW MANY ARE ENOUGH?

Repetitions are the building blocks of a strength program. The choice of a rep range represents the first step in deciding the direction your program will follow.

In strength training, as in fitness and other training modes, intensity relative to a maximum, that is, training at different levels of your maximum strength, produces different results. The different levels of your maximum strength can be divided into training zones that allow you to select the repetition range appropriate for the goal you are trying to achieve. When trained accurately, each zone will produce a particular physiological response. Theoretically this makes the selection of a repetition range quite simple as you need only match up your preferred goal with the appropriate rep range. However, efficient strength programs are a little more complex. Read on…

ESTIMATED 1RM = A X ((0.0367 X B) +0.9508)

Where: A = Load, B = Reps

Example:
Squat 6 @ 110kg (therefore A = 110, B = 6)
Then… 110 x ((0.0367 x 6) + 0.9508)
         110 x (0.2202 + 0.9508)
         110 x 1.171
         = 128.81 (round down to nearest 2.5kg = 127.5kg)

TRAIN TOUGH

This table shows the general goals/outcomes of each repetition range.

The number one thing to remember when selecting a rep range is there is no magic number. No single repetition range will work for every person all the time. The most effective training is achieved using a mixture of reps at different times throughout your program.

Two rules of thumb are:

1 As the weight gets heavier, reps get lower.

2 As the weight gets lighter, the reps go up.

TRAINING ZONE	% OF IRM	REPS	EFFECT
Maximum strength	100% 97% 95% 92%	1 2 3 4	Increased neural efficiency. Increased inter- and intra-muscular coordination. Stimulation of Type II (b) muscle fibres.
Optimisation of maximum strength and hypertrophy	89% 86% 83%	5 6 7	Increased neural efficiency. Increased protein turnover. Stimulation of Type II(a) and some Type II(b) muscle fibres.
Hypertrophy	80% 77% 75%	8 9 10 11 12	Increased rate of protein turnover leading to hypertrophy (growth). Stimulation of Type II(a) muscle fibres.
Strength endurance		13	Alteration in muscular biochemistry allowing for continued work in increasingly acidic environment.

WORD FROM THE COACH

At all times during a strength session you need to be switched on to the technical aspects of what you are doing. It is not enough to just lift the weight. If it is not lifted correctly (both in technique and intensity) you expose yourself to unnecessary risk or reduced training efficiency.

Be aware of the following things.
- Technique must be maintained at all times.

- If the weight selected results in technique breakdown, the weight is too heavy and must be reduced.

- If the weight selected does not cause a degree of fatigue then the load should be increased.

TYPES OF STRENGTH TRAINING PROGRAMS

Anatomical adaptation

In the initial stages of a strength training program the muscles, tendons and joints of the body must be allowed time to adapt to the increased load. This period of adaptation is crucial to an injury free state in this and other phases of training. Anatomical adaptation or general physical preparation (GPP) programs typically consist of basic low-load exercises that recruit the major muscle groups of the body in a pattern similar to the way in which they will be used in later, more intensive training.

Strength endurance

Endurance programs are based around developing the muscles' ability to contract over an extended period, generally 1–3 min against low–medium resistance. This attribute is developed in sports like rowing and wrestling. Muscle endurance training also forms the basis for some programs aimed at decreasing fat through stimulation of the metabolic rate and numerous lipolytic (fat-burning) enzymes.

Hypertrophy

Hypertrophy programs are aimed solely at increasing the cross sectional area of the targeted muscle, that is, 'pumping up'. There are numerous effective methods of generating muscle hypertrophy, many of which are discussed throughout *Train Tough*. One of the most important lessons to be learned when using these varied techniques is 'what works for you'. While you should constantly aim to achieve a degree of variety in your training, it is always good to know those 'go to' techniques that you can use with confidence.

Maximum strength

Maximum strength methods are aimed at improving the efficiency of the neuromuscular system via increased rate of muscle fibre 'firing' and coordination of the recruitment patterns within and between muscles.

Power

The objective of power training is to increase the speed at which you can apply force. This branch of training is aimed at increasing the acceleration part of the force equation. In general, a lighter load is lifted with the intention of moving the weight as fast as possible. There are a number of specific techniques that may be employed to achieve an increase in power (some of which are beyond the scope of *Train Tough*).

One of the most accepted ways to increase power in modern sport is by utilising various forms of Olympic-style lifting, for example, Power Cleans. The effectiveness of these techniques when applied to sport in general has been overstated to some degree. While the development of power from these lifts can be exceptional it is critical that the correct technique be used, which in many sports does not happen. Lack of correct technique will reduce the effectiveness of the exercises. Make sure that if you follow programs including Olympic-style lifts you spend time with a quality coach to develop a sound technique.

TRAIN TOUGH

GENERAL PRINCPLES OF STRENGTH TRAINING

Now you have the basics of strength training under your belt and are no doubt busting to start on your own program. However, take a breath and have a look at the general principles of strength training. They'll give you a bit of structure to develop your training to suit your individual needs.

Train large muscle groups before small muscle groups

Large muscle groups are simply those that contain the greatest level of muscle tissue. For example, Bench Press before Tricep Pushdowns – Bench Press recruits the pectorals, shoulders, triceps and lats, while the Tricep Pushdown recruits the triceps. This principle can be used in pre-exhaustion sets (detailed in Chapter 14, 'Sealed section') designed to specifically target single muscles.

Don't always train to fatigue

Every session you complete should not be done to complete fatigue. Try to target one session per week to really open up on yourself. Other sessions should then be done at a slightly lower intensity. Again, as with many elements of training, this guideline can be manipulated to achieve different results in more advanced programs.

Maintain strict technique at all times

Don't risk injuries. The gym is a place to get stronger and improve your personal performance in your chosen field. Don't risk injuries by using techniques that you are unfamiliar with, or using techniques incorrectly.

Keep a training journal

This is really important. To continue to improve it is essential to keep an accurate record of the training you have completed so that you can make adjustments in your training to help you move forward. I have seen many athletes over the years convince themselves that they are training really well when in fact they haven't made any significant improvements in their last 12 months of training.

Use recovery/unloading cycles

Effective training is based on applying a training stimulus and then allowing appropriate recovery to achieve increased performance. This format applies from session to session, week to week, month to month. Use these guidelines to apply recovery cycles:

Have at least one day off per week.

Have 1 easy (recovery) week every 3–6 weeks. More experienced athletes require more recovery weeks more frequently, while less experienced athletes benefit more from longer training cycles (4–6 weeks) between recovery weeks.

Vary your training regularly

Variety is the key to the universe. Changing different elements of your program on a regular basis will force your body to adapt to the new stimulus and open the way for improvement. Variety, as with many other elements of training, is really dictated by experience. The greater your training experience the more regularly you need to make changes; conversely, the less your experience the greater time required before you need to make changes.

- Beginner–intermediate lifters should change one exercise at least every 3–4 weeks, with changes in rep ranges every 4–6 weeks.

- Intermediate to advanced lifters should vary a minimum of 1–2 exercises every fortnight, with rep range changes every 2–3 weeks.

STRENGTH WARM UP

One of the most neglected parts of any strength program is the warm up. Few people, if any, really take the time to prepare their bodies for the session. It's quite common to see guys lob in to the gym, take a moment to survey the available equipment and then launch into an intensive work set without having done a single stretch.

Compare this to the program of a competitive athlete, who may take 30–40 min to warm-up. This is particularly obvious with track and field athletes, most notably sprinters. Why would a sprinter need to warm up the longest? Because they train at a very high intensity all the time.

To maintain training performance and to stay injury-free, a thorough warm up is critical. So, how long should you warm up before you start on training?

A good rule of thumb is the length of the warm up should be proportional to the session's intensity. That is, the higher the intensity, the longer the warm up.

Effective warm ups can prepare you for high intensity sessions. As with the major components of your program (strength, fitness, and so on) the warm up only needs a small amount of direction to improve training. The warm up should increase your body temperature before starting your training session.

This achieves a number of things:

- Increases blood flow (and therefore oxygen and nutrients) to the muscles. More oxygen equals greater capacity for energy supply and removal of waste products.

- Lubricants flow around the joints improving function and protecting joint surfaces.

- Muscle tissue contractile rates are higher and more powerful due to an increase in neural efficiency (the rate at which the brain fires the muscles).

- Muscular contractions are sustained for longer as a result of effective removal of waste products.

TRAIN TOUGH

When are you warmed up enough?

The body functions within a safe physiological limit so that your body temperature will only vary within a few degrees. Taking your body temperature beyond the safe limit will be detrimental to performance, not to mention your health. The easiest way to work out when your body is getting to the correct temperature is by your perspiration rate. As you heat up, your body starts sweating to cool down. The appearance of a light sweat is a pretty good sign that you're warm.

While increasing body temperature is critical to the warm up it is not the only element. The use of dynamic flexibility drills will increase the range of movement around a joint and improve its function. This form of flexibility reduces the effects of residual fatigue by assisting the muscle to return to its correct functional length. The reason for including flexibility in the warm up is to prepare for the session ahead. Making larger scale changes to your flexibility requires specific time set aside to facilitate that change. Everybody, especially as you get older, should dedicate time to maintaining a good functional length in all major muscle groups (see Chapter 10, 'Flexibility').

METHODS OF MAINTAINING MECHANICAL STRESS

CLUSTER SETS

Cluster sets are based on the manipulation of recovery phases within a set. Each repetition of a cluster set is broken up by a short pause, a small window of recovery, which allows you to lift a greater load.

Exercise: Squat

1RM: 200 kg

Normal set: 4 x 6 reps @ 160 kg

Cluster set:
- Rep 1 @ 170 kg
- 10 second rest (rack the bar)
- Rep 2 @ 170 kg
- 10 sec rest (rack the bar)
- Continue up to 6 reps
- Rep 6 @ 170 kg
- 3 min rest then repeat 2–3 times

The lesson: The same number of reps has been completed but with 10 kg more weight. Therefore the mechanical stress placed on the muscle has been significantly increased.

DROP SETS

These work on the idea that by using a higher load in the earlier sets you recruit and fatigue the high threshold motor units (FT(b) fibres) before fatiguing the remaining muscle fibres. This operates in a sort of flow-on effect as you reduce the load in the follow on sets.

Exercise: Incline Bench Press

1RM: 150 kg

Normal set: 4 x 6 reps @ 122.5 kg

Drop set:
- 4 x 2 reps @ 135 kg (get your training partner to remove 5 kg)
- 4 x 2 reps @ 130 kg (get your training partner to remove 10 kg)
- 4 x 2 reps @ 120 kg
- 4 x 3–4 min recovery

DECLINE SETS

Decline sets are not dissimilar from drop sets except that they drop intensity across sets, not repetitions. The objective of the decline set is to stay within the repetition range starting with the highest load possible for the lowest reps, then progressively reducing the weight and increasing the reps completed. The main thing to note is that each set needs to be completed at or very near to fatigue.

Exercise: Incline Bench Press

1RM: 150 kg

Normal set: 4 x 6 reps @ 122.5 kg

Decline set: 6 reps @ 130 kg (maximum effort), followed by a 3 minute recovery
- 4–6 reps @ 125 kg (maximum effort), followed by a 3 min recovery
- 4–6 reps @ 120 kg (maximum effort), followed by a 3 min recovery
- 4–6 reps @ 115 kg (maximum effort)

And for the courageous ones:

Exercise: Chin-ups

Drop set: 1 x 4 reps with 30 kg strapped on, followed by a 2 min recovery
- 1 x 6 reps with 20 kg strapped on, followed by a 2 min recovery
- 1 x 8 reps with 10 kg strapped on, followed by a 2 min recovery
- 1 x maximum reps with no weight.

TRAIN TOUGH

METHODS OF MAINTAINING TIME UNDER TENSION

LIFTING SPEED

All lifts are broken down into three major parts:

1 Eccentric contraction
As the muscle develops force and lengthens, the weight is lowered.

2 Isometric contraction
The pause at the bottom of the movement is where the muscle develops force but does not move.

3 Concentric contraction
The commonly described 'flexing' of the muscle where force is developed, the muscle shortens and the weight is lifted up.

Slowing down the execution speed of any of these parts within the lift increases the time that the muscle is subjected to the stress of the weight. That's a good thing. However, reducing the weight significantly in order to increase the time-under-tension will reduce the mechanical stress on the muscle. That's a bad thing.

Partial repetitions increase the amount of time each rep takes.

Manipulating the execution of lifts like this may be done to major exercises such as:

- Squat
- Front Squat
- Split Squat
- Bench Press (including incline, decline and close grip variations)
- Dips
- Military Press

For example:
Squat 11/2:
- Start in the normal position
- Squat in the bottom position
- Drive up into a half squat and pause
- Squat back down to the bottom position
- Drive back to the finishing position

NUTS AND BOLTS
7 STRENGTH EXERCISES AND MORE

The exercises included here are based on the training systems developed in the weight-lifting empires of the former Soviet Union and Bulgaria. In these systems, all lifting is based around the *fundamental* lifts, with extra work generated using *variation* lifts and *additional* lifts. Exercises in this chapter give you all the bricks you need to build the wall of your training program.

Fundamental lifts involve movements engaging multiple muscle groups and joint structures working together in a coordinated pattern. Lifts of this nature are often referred to as whole body lifts. Their effectiveness is based on the fact that they recruit the greatest amount of muscle mass (multiple muscle groups) in a coordinated manner. Fundamental lifts, because of their complex requirements, are effective at replicating the movement pattern of basic athletic elements (running, jumping, and so on). All good for getting you ready for a more athletic training program.

A VERY IMPORTANT TRAINING TIP

A neutral position or neutral spine refers to the position your spine would be in if you were to stand 'to attention' like a soldier on parade with your chest held up, shoulderblades back and down, and your abdominal wall braced. This position should be held throughout all major movements.

FUNDAMENTAL LIFTS

1 Squat
Muscle groups: butt (glutes), hamstrings, quads, inner thigh (adductor).

Set Up
- Stand tall with your feet about shoulder width apart with your toes pointed forward or turned slightly out (about a 25-degree angle).

- Position the bar comfortably on the back of your shoulders, behind and below your neck. (Tip: you should feel as if you are holding the load through your upper back not the base of your neck.) With your hands on the bar, rotate your elbows under the bar, pointing towards the floor. This will also help hold the 'chest up' position.

- Balance your body weight evenly over both feet. (Avoid feeling the weight predominantly through the front of the foot.)

- Keep your chest held up, shoulderblades back and down, which will create a natural platform for the bar.

The Descent

■ Take a breath, tighten your abdominal muscles and brace your abdominal wall.

■ Shift your hips back slightly to initiate the movement. Your movements should be smooth and controlled.

■ Keep your chest up as you sit down into the Squat.

■ Make sure your weight is felt through the middle to back of the foot, not the front.

■ A full squat is completed when the hip has been lowered below the knee. This is the optimum squat depth. You may need to start out using a shallower depth in order to practise your skill and gain confidence.

■ Your level of flexibility will affect the range of movement. Your ankles and hamstrings need to be fairly flexible. (See the training tips on p 55.)

The Lift

- Drive from your hips, as if you were trying to push through your shoulders. Don't bounce at the bottom of the squat to get the impetus to come up.

- Squeeze your glutes to initiate the return journey.

Repeat the mantra 'suck, sit, squeeze' to remember the key elements of the Squat

- Suck air in and brace against your abs.
- Sit into the Squat.
- Squeeze your glutes to get out of the bottom position.

Variations:
Split Squat

Do this the same way as the Squat but the catch is … you do the Squat on one leg.

- Place one leg forward, and stretch the other leg behind you with just the toes touching the ground.

- Slowly bend the front leg, moving into the squat position. The leg that is behind you is for balance only. All the weight should be through the foot of the front leg.

- The descent is identical to that of the squat with a focus on feeling the weight through the heel and squeezing through the glutes in the bottom position.

Front Squat

Develops strength and range of movement for the Clean and Power Clean movements.

■ This lift is practised in the same way as a squat except that the bar is rested across the front of the shoulders

■ Bar positioning:
   • Bar should sit high on the shoulders, across the top of the collarbones.
   • Elbows should be pushed up to allow the bar to sit naturally on the platform created by the anterior (front) deltoids (or shoulder muscles).

SUCK, SIT, SQUEEZE

TRAINING TIPS

Hold your breath until your return to the starting position. Breathing out decreases the intra-abdominal pressure and therefore the rigidity of the connection between your upper and lower body.

If your range of movement does not allow a full squat, use the steps below with lighter weights for a few weeks.

■ Religiously complete bent Leg Calf Stretch (see Chapter 10, 'Flexibility'). Hold for 60 sec minimum with 3–4 reps, 8–10 times per day.

■ Use heel chocks to allow greater range of motion. (Place a 5 cm block of wood or a 5 kg plate under your heels). This will help you achieve greater depth in the squat (most people are limited in squat range by calf flexibility). The chocks will make you feel like you want to fall forward, so it is critically important that you keep your weight firmly down on your heels. When starting to use this technique make sure that your load is vastly reduced until you are confident with the change of position. This technique should be used in conjunction with the calf stretch and conventional squats in order to improve range of movement to allow correct full squatting.

TRAIN TOUGH

Additional lifts:
THE LUNGE

Essentially a variation on the Split Squat which comes in three formats.

Static Lunge

■ As for the Split Squat with the rear foot elevated off the ground (typically on a bench or box).

■ Those with poor quad flexibility will struggle in this exercise. Try starting on a box about half the height of your shin and work your way up to approximately knee height.

■ Focus all the weight loading through your front foot not the back foot.

■ Keep elbows under the bar and drive the hips up under the bar.

■ This is a great variation to focus technique on the front leg.

■ Static Lunge is often used by field athletes (shot put, discus, etc) as a variation to heavy squatting. (Lifting at the same intensity in a Static Lunge as in a Squat requires roughly half the total load. This reduces stress on the back significantly when these exercises are employed 2–3 times per week.)

Dynamic Lunge

■ The execution of this lift is similar to the Split Squat with the starting position as for the conventional Squat.

■ Step forward to initiate the lift. Beginners should aim to step forward approximately 25–50 per cent of their standing height, while more advanced individuals can push out beyond this to approximately 75 per cent of their standing height.

■ As you go into the lunge, focus on solid foot placement (that is, controlled balance, not wobbling all over the place).

■ Keep your torso upright throughout this lift.

■ Press back into the original standing position.

Walking Lunge

■ The execution is similar to that of the Dynamic Lunge. Instead of pushing back to the start position, drive yourself up and forward, establishing a new starting position, a step in front of where you started (hence the name).

■ The key to this exercise is driving your hips up and through on the step forward. Don't shoot your arse out the back and then pull your body back over a straight leg.

TRAINING TIP
Start out completing this exercise with just your body weight, then add external resistance once you have mastered the technique. It is easy to get this one wrong by loading too much too early.

TRAINING TIP
As you step out imagine that you are stepping over a box, then drive your leg over the box as you press back to the start position. This will keep your leg action high, producing a greater focus on recruiting the glutes to get out of the bottom position.

2 Deadlift

Muscle groups: hamstrings, butt (glutes), lower back (erector spinae).

Set Up

■ Stand tall with your feet about shoulder width apart and toes turned out slightly.

■ Your shins should be very close to the bar or lightly touching it when you bend your knees and lower your hips to prepare for the lift.

■ Grip the bar slightly wider than shoulder-width with your palms facing towards you. Your arms should be outside your knees and your neck should be held in a neutral position, which means you look neither up nor down.

■ The lift must start with the hips down and your spine straight. Hold your chest up and make sure it faces the wall in front of you.

■ Pull your shoulderblades together and then down your back. This will help maintain a neutral spine which is critical to do this lift safely.

■ Your shoulders should be over or slightly ahead of the bar.

■ Inhale before you lift the bar to ensure a tight torso (exactly the same technique as described for the Squat). This increases the intra-abdominal pressure and offers greater support to the lower portion of the spine.

The Lift

- As you stand with the weight, imagine pushing the floor away from you with your feet. Make the lift a smooth, slow, easy pull off the floor.

- Your hips and shoulders rise together at the same rate.

- The bar should come up straight and stay close to the body.

- Keep your arms straight, shoulderblades back, shoulders over the bar, and make sure neutral spine is maintained.

- Your head and eyes should remain facing forward.

The Descent

- Bend at the knees and hips, and follow the same path as the lift, but perform the movements in reverse, as you bring the bar to the floor.

- Maintain the position of your back, that is, shoulderblades pulled together and down, chest held up and high.

TRAINING TIP

As the loads get heavier, it is OK to drop the bar from the top position, which will eliminate the lowering part of the lift. As the Deadlift focuses on the raising part of the lift, this will reduce the total load on your back, while at the same time allowing you to apply a solid training stimulus.

Additional lifts:
Back Extensions

- Using a Back Extension bench, position yourself so that your hips are aligned just over the edge of the bench and both legs are secured under the leg supports.

- These lifts should always be completed with the chest held high and shoulderblades held back and down.

- The movement should occur from the hips, not the back. The back must remain in a neutral position throughout the movement.

TRAIN TOUGH

- A full range of movement should be used but the upper body should only be lifted until it is in line with the lower body (that is, horizontal to the ground).

- Do not bounce at the bottom of the lift.

TRAINING TIPS

Looking for more intensity? If ordinary Back Extensions are becoming easy try these progressions (listed in order of difficulty).

- Extend one or both arms above your head at the top of the movement.

- Hold a medicine ball or plate against your chest (start very light).

- Hold a medicine ball or plate above your head in the top position of the movement.

- Place a larger load on your back using a conventional bar. (Only for extremely experienced trainers. Not to be taken lightly!)

Single Leg Back Extensions

- The technique is the same as for the Back Extensions with the exception that only one leg is secured.

3 Good Morning

Muscle groups: hamstrings, butt (glutes), lower back (erector spinae).

Set Up
- As for the Squat.

The Descent
- Keep your chest up and shoulderblades back and down. This will create a natural platform for the bar. This positioning of the shoulders and chest needs to be held throughout this lift.

- Take a breath, tighten your abdominal muscles and brace against your abdomen.

- The lift begins by pushing the hips back and allowing the shoulders to come forward. Your movements should be smooth and controlled.

- Knees must be kept slightly bent through the entire lift.

- Keep your weight pressing down through the back of your foot.

- Your centre of gravity should remain over your feet with your hips moving back and your shoulders moving forward to help you with balance.

- Your head should be kept in line with your spine throughout the movement (some of you might feel the urge to lift your head and arch your neck back to initiate the movement – this is a big *no-no*!).

- When this lift is done correctly you should feel a stretch/working sensation in each hamstring.

TRAINING TIP
If you continue to allow your knees to bend the load will come off your hamstrings and will move into the quads. Maintain a slight bend in the knees at all times and focus on pushing your butt back over your heels.

TRAIN TOUGH

The Lift
- To complete the lift drive the hips back to the starting position, focusing on using the hamstrings to haul the upper body up.

TRAINING TIPS
- Some people may find it more comfortable to use a low-bar position in the Good Morning. You can do this by allowing the bar to sit further back on your shoulders than in a conventional Squat position.

- Avoid going beyond the horizontal position as gravity dictates that the bar will want to push down onto your neck, which will make for a painful lift.

Additional lifts:
The Romanian Deadlift
The perfect complement to the Good Morning.
- Start in the top position as for the Deadlift. Your knees should be bent slightly as in the movement for the Good Morning.

- Do the lift the same as the Good Morning by shifting the hips back and allowing your shoulders to move forward. Keep your chest high with shoulderblades back and down.

- Your arms need to be kept straight throughout the lift. Hold the load and don't try to lift it with your arms.

- The bar should move in a vertical line straight down finishing just above the knee cap (higher if your flexibility is poor).

- Complete the lift by driving the hips back to the start position, visualising the hamstrings hauling the upper body up (same as for the Good Morning).

The Single Leg Romanian Deadlift

This is a further variation, which may be completed with either a bar or dumbbells.

■ Set up as for the conventional Romanian Deadlift, except that you stand on one leg.

■ All the same techniques apply as for the conventional Romanian Deadlift.

TRAIN TOUGH

Natural Glute–Ham Raise

This is a specific and very demanding exercise for the glutes, hamstrings, and calves.

■ Kneel on the ground and have a partner hold your ankles to the ground.

■ Lower your body forward while maintaining a straight line from your ear to your knee (this means that you have to lower yourself by allowing your knees to extend/open up).

■ Lower yourself as far as you can, then allow yourself to drop to the ground landing in a push-up position (you're still on your knees here).

■ For the beginner/intermediate version work on lowering yourself with as much control as possible, and drop to the push-up position when you reach your limit.

TRAINING TIPS

This exercise may also be done in two other ways.

■ Riding solo – hook your heels under a low bench if you don't have a training partner.

■ Use a glute ham bench – these can be found in athlete-orientated gyms as opposed to commercial set ups. The bench is similar to a back extension bench except that the main pad is round and the feet are placed in specific chocks. If you think you have access to a bench like this make sure a qualified coach runs you through how to use it.

Looking for something a little harder?

■ After lowering yourself to the ground, hold the straight-line body position and push up hard with your upper body, ideally to approximately halfway back to the start position.

■ At this point you will need to contract your hamstrings to finish the movement back to the starting position.

■ Any gurus out there can try lowering and raising themselves using just their hamstrings – tough but not impossible.

4 Chin-up

Muscle groups: Lats, shoulderblade retractors, shoulders (posterior deltoids), biceps, brachialis and forearm muscles.

■ The basic Chin-up may be done with an underhand grip (supinated, where you grip underneath the bar) or an overhand grip (pronated, where you grip over the bar).

■ The grip changes the focus on particular muscles:

- The underhand grip tends to work the elbow flexors (bicep, etc), and develops thickness in the lats.
- A close overhand grip loads the elbow flexors in the forearm, and the biceps and contributes to development of thickness in the lats.
- A wide overhand grip loads the lats to a greater extent.

■ Starting from a hanging position, lift your body until your upper chest touches the bar (at this point your chin should be well over the bar).

■ Slowly return to the starting position. Don't swing backwards and forwards while doing this.

■ The beauty of this exercise is its absolute simplicity – just hang on and lift.

TRAINING TIPS

■ When lifting up, try to visualise that you are pulling your elbows into your ribs. This may sound strange but it will pinpoint your focus on lifting from your upper back rather than from your arms.

■ Try gripping the bar with a mixed grip (one hand over, and one under) for something different.

■ Loop a towel over the bar and hold it in one hand to add a more difficult gripping element to the lift (try two if you want to really go hard).

TRAIN TOUGH

Additional lifts:
Bent Over Row

■ Stand with a barbell in front of you and your feet shoulder-width apart, knees slightly bent.

■ Bend forward at the waist and push your hips back a bit until your torso is almost parallel to the floor. (Your arms should hang straight down.)

■ Your chest should be held up with shoulderblades back and down making sure your have a neutral spine position.

■ Use an overhand grip on the bar, about shoulder-width apart.

■ Slowly pull the barbell towards your chest, just below your pecs. Don't use upper body movement to help you with the lift. Pause and then slowly lower the bar to the floor.

TRAINING TIPS

■ For variation the grip on the bar may be made narrow or wide, while the orientation of the grip may also be changed to underhand.

■ This lift may also be done using dumbbells.

■ Single Arm Bent Over Row is completed using one arm only, which forces your body to stabilise through the abdominals. (It may be done with one knee on a bench. I like to use this to challenge my core stability by using no support and bracing strongly through the abdominals.)

■ This lift may be pushed a little further by using an Olympic bar in one hand (experienced lifters only need apply).

5 Bench Press

Muscle groups: Chest (pectoralis major and minor), shoulders (anterior deltoid), triceps and lats

Set Up

- Lie on your back on a bench with your feet flat on the floor slightly wider than shoulder-width apart.

> **TRAINING TIP**
>
> Some coaches advocate the elevating of the feet (some up on a bench, some off the ground altogether). While there may be some limited arguments for this approach (elements of injury rehabilitation is certainly one), if you are serious about trying to improve performance stick to the basic method as it provides a better base from which to launch your press.

- Your upper back and glutes (butt muscles) should be the two points of contact on the bench, with the natural curve in your lower back leaving a small gap between it and the bench. Don't try to flatten your back against the bench.

- Draw your shoulderblades back and down along your spine. Your chest should be held high. While this primarily gives you the greatest stability when pressing, it also reduces the distance from the bar to your chest, which helps when you are lifting heavy loads.

- Regardless of the handgrip, rotate your elbows in at the start of the lift. This serves to align the triceps in a more favourable position for recruitment. Allowing your elbows to rotate out places a greater load on the front of your shoulder and may lead to reduced efficiency at the 'sticking point'. Keeping the elbows in basically allows you to blast through the sticking point.

The Descent

- Lower the bar to your lower rib area.

- As with other fundamental lifts, when lifting heavy, take a breath at the top position and brace hard through your abs.

The Lift

- Maintaining your breath hold and brace, prepare to start the lift phase just as the bar is approaching your chest. This will help increase your speed at the bottom position (being slow out of the bottom position will kill you).

- Lift the barbell upwards in a straight line off the chest. Try to visualise pushing your body into the bench and away from the bar, rather than pressing the bar off your chest.

- Push hard against your abs and continue to hold your breath. Letting your breath out will reduce your intra-abdominal pressure and thereby reduce the base from which you can push.

- Keep your elbows under the bar to maximise the work of the triceps.

> **TRAINING TIPS**
>
> - When pressing heavier weights always use a spotter.
>
> - When nearing the end of a maximum effort don't go looking for the rack as it will cause you to push the bar in an arc back toward the racks rather than up in a straight line. Stay focused on the skill, maintain body position and get those elbows locked out.

Variations:
Incline/Decline Bench Press

■ Changes in position of the upper body in the Bench Press alters the activation of the pecs. For example, the more inclined the bench becomes the greater the activation of the upper portions of the pecs and the shoulders; the more declined the bench, the greater the activation of the lower portions of the pecs and the triceps. You'll be weaker the higher the incline becomes and stronger the greater the decline becomes.

Close/Wide Grip

■ Changes in the width of the grip will alter the contribution of the pecs and tricep muscles. For example, closer grips work a greater proportion of the triceps; wider grips work a greater proportion of the pectorals.

Floor Press

■ Do this the same way as for the Bench Press, but lie on the floor.

■ Have a spotter lift the bar into the starting position for you.

■ Lower the bar until your elbows touch the ground. Then press back to the start position.

■ This exercise emphasises the use of the triceps in the final section of the Bench Press. It can be a useful exercise to put into your program when you need to take the load off the shoulders for a period of time.

68

Additional lifts:
Dumbbell (DB) variations

■ Dumbbells may be used for any of the variations above. Keep in mind that dumbbells are less stable than a bar, therefore you will be required to reduce total load for any given rep range.

■ Turning dumbbells so that the thumbs point towards your head will use the triceps to a greater extent. Rotating the dumbbells so that the thumbs point toward the middle of the body will increase the chest (pecs) activity.

Dips

■ Dips are fantastic for triceps and chest (pecs) development.

■ Using bars that are closer together increases the movement of the triceps, while wider bars accentuate the use of the chest (pecs) muscles.

■ Don't be scared to throw on a dipping belt or lash a bit of weight to your body for some extra overload.

■ Grip the handles and push yourself to a starting position, keeping your arms and torso straight.

■ With your elbows close to your body and keeping your hips straight, lower your body until the shoulders are slightly stretched. Avoid going so deep that you think your shoulders are going to pop.

■ Push your body up into the starting position and repeat. You can do the dips with bent or straight legs.

TRAINING TIP
Anyone who has had a shoulder reconstruction or other significant shoulder capsule injury should avoid the use of dips because of the stress placed on the front part of the joint capsule.

6 Power Clean

Muscle groups: butt (glutes), hamstrings, quads, calves.

Set Up (as for Deadlift)

- Stand tall with your feet about shoulder-width apart and toes turned out slightly.

- Your shins should be very close to the bar or lightly touching it when you bend your knees and lower your hips to prepare for the lift.

- Grip the bar slightly wider than shoulder-width with your palms facing towards you. Your arms should be outside your knees and your neck should be held in a neutral position, which means you look neither up nor down.

- The lift must start with the hips down and your spine straight. Hold your chest up and make sure it faces the wall in front of you.

- Pull your shoulderblades together and then down your back. This will help maintain a 'neutral' spine, which is critical to do this lift safely.

The First Pull (from the floor to the knees)

- Inhale and brace before you start the first pull.

- As you stand with the weight, imagine pushing the floor away from you with your feet. Make the lift a smooth, slow, easy pull off the floor.

- Your hips and shoulders should rise together at the same rate, while keeping the angle of the back constant.

- The bar should come up straight and stay close to the legs.

- Keep your arms straight, your shoulders back and above the bar and be really aware of maintaining a neutral spine.

- Your head and eyes should remain facing forward.

The Second Pull
(from the knees to the squat under)

- Keep thinking neutral spine as you drive your hips forwards toward the bar while the shoulders are shrugged to the ears simultaneously (Speed Shrug). Move the bar explosively once it reaches your thighs, by extending your knee, hip and ankle joints in a jumping action, and come up onto your toes. The bar should be moving fairly close to the body at this point.

- As the bar accelerates the legs are fully extended.

- Your arms should remain straight until the last instant when the body is fully extended. Then they can bend as you draw the bar up to about mid-chest.

The Squat Under (getting under the bar)
- As the bar is drawn up to the chest, drop your body under the bar into a shallow Front Squat position.

- As your elbows are driven under the bar, keep them pointing forward.

- In the final position, the bar is caught across the front of the shoulders (in a Front Squat position). Make sure you flex your hips and knees to absorb the weight of the bar and then push yourself to a standing position.

Lowering the bar
- If you are new to this lift, the bar may be returned to the ground by lowering the bar off the chest, and then down to the floor.

- More experienced lifters using heavier loads should simply press up slightly using the legs, and as the bar moves off the chest drop your elbows, take the arms from under the bar and let the weight drop to the ground under control.

TRAINING TIPS
- Before attempting to lift a loaded bar, practise the correct technique using a broomstick and progress slowly to an unloaded bar.

- Always use the right equipment. Using non-Olympic bars (that is, bars not designed to spin) will end in tears and injury.

- The Power Clean technique is quite complex but very rewarding. Take your time practising each element separately (investing in a coach would advance your technique quickly).

- **Back care:** This lift, when executed correctly, is completely safe. Performing it incorrectly or with load beyond your skill is a recipe for disaster. If this book has stimulated your interest sufficiently to pursue this exercise in detail, ensure you get a qualified coach to work through the skill with you.

Variations:
Hang Clean

- The Hang Clean is a component of the Power Clean and may be used as an independent exercise.

- It is a good drill to practise the explosive Second Pull and the Squat Under.

- All technical elements of the Hang Clean are the same as for the Power Clean except that the starting position is with the bar hanging just on top of the knee caps, rather than on the floor (see Power Clean Hang on p 70).

The Lift

- Keep thinking neutral spine as you drive your hips forwards toward the bar while the shoulders are shrugged to the ears simultaneously (Speed Shrug). Move the bar explosively once it reaches your thighs, by extending your knee, hip and ankle joints in a jumping action, and come up onto your toes. The bar should be moving fairly close to the body at this point.

- As the bar accelerates the legs are fully extended.

- Your arms should remain straight until the last instant when the body is fully extended. Then they can bend as you draw the bar up to about mid-chest.

The Squat Under (getting under the bar)

- As the bar is drawn up to the chest, drop your body under the bar into a shallow Front Squat position.

- As your elbows are driven under the bar, keep them pointing forward.

- In the final position, the bar is caught across the front of the shoulders (in a Front Squat position). Make sure you flex your hips and knees to absorb the weight of the bar and then push yourself to a standing position.

- Lower the bar using the same technique as for the Power Clean.

The Clean Pull

- The Clean Pull is a component of the Power Clean that may be used as an independent exercise.

- The start position is the same as for the Power Clean.

- The Clean Pull focuses on the first and second pull of the Power Clean.

- The lift is complete when the bar reaches chest height.

- The bar is not taken into the Squat Under position, but is returned to the ground for the next repetition.

7 Power Snatch

Muscle groups: butt (glutes), hamstrings, quads, calves.

Set Up

- Stand with feet flat on the floor, about shoulder-width apart and toes pointed slightly outward.

- Your shins should be very close to the bar or lightly touching it when you bend your knees and lower your hips to prepare for the lift.

- Grip the bar approximately 10–15 cm wider than your shoulders on each side.

- Your neck should be held in a neutral position, which means you look neither up nor down.

- The lift must start with the hips down while keeping your spine straight. Hold your chest up and facing forwards.

- Pull your shoulderblades together and then down. This will maintain a neutral spine, which is critical for safe execution.

The First Pull (from the floor to the knees)

- Inhale and brace before you start the first pull.

- As you stand up with the weight, imagine pushing the earth away from you with your feet. Make the lift a smooth, slow, easy pull off the floor.

- Your hips and shoulders rise together at the same rate, while keeping the angle of the back constant.

- The bar should come up straight and stay close to the legs.

- Keep your arms straight, shoulders back and above the bar, neutral spine maintained.

- Your head and eyes should remain facing forward.

TRAIN TOUGH

The Second Pull (from the knees to the squat under)

■ Maintain a neutral spine at all times.

■ Drive your hips forward towards the bar while the shoulders are shrugged to the ears simultaneously (Speed Shrug). Move the bar explosively once it reaches your thighs, by extending your knee, hip and ankle joints in a jumping action, and come up onto your toes. The bar should be moving fairly close to the body at this point.

■ As the bar accelerates the legs are fully extended.

■ Your arms should remain straight until the last instant when the body is fully extended. Then they can bend as you draw the bar up to about mid-chest.

The Squat Under (getting under the bar)

■ As the bar is drawn up to the chest, the body is dropped under the bar into a Squat position, catching the bar above the head with locked arms.

Lowering the bar

■ If you are new to this lift, the bar may be returned to the ground by lowering the bar off the chest, and then down to the floor.

■ More experienced lifters using heavier loads should simply press up slightly using the legs, and as the bar moves off the chest drop your elbows, take the arms from under the bar and let the weight drop to the ground under control.

NOTHING BEATS A PROFESSIONAL COACH. IF YOU ARE SERIOUS ... GET ONE!

TRAINING TIPS

■ Starting with the bar in the overhead (squat under) position and squatting down while maintaining the bar in position is called an Overhead Squat. This is a good learning tool to establish an awareness of where the bar has to be positioned above you in order to be balanced. Use this exercise in the early stages of learning to become familiar with bar positioning.

■ Once you feel comfortable with the Overhead Squat, have a crack at the full technique using a broomstick to avoid injury. If you are unsure as to how to progress seek qualified assistance.

Variations:

Hang Snatch

- The Hang Snatch is a component of the Power Snatch that may be used as an independent exercise.

- It is a good learning drill to practise the explosive Second Pull and the Squat Under by using the Hang Snatch.

- All technical elements of the Hang Snatch are the same as for the Power Snatch except that the starting position is with the bar hanging just on top of the knee caps (Power Snatch Hang Above).

The Snatch Pull

- Again, the Snatch Pull is a component of the Power Snatch that may be used as an independent exercise. The bar is not taken into the Squat Under position, but is returned to the floor for the next position.

- The Snatch Pull focuses on the first and second pull of the Power Snatch.

- The lift is complete when the bar reaches chest height.

Additional lifts:

Dumbbell (DB) Snatch

- Is completed with one arm in the 'hang' position (above the knee cap).

- Drive up from the hips, drawing the dumbbell to the chest toward the end of the movement.

- As the dumbbell gets to chest height, squat under the dumbbell and catch the weight with a locked arm.

- This is a great conditioning drill and a good substitute when there are no facilities for a conventional Power Snatch.

TRAIN TOUGH

The Single Arm Snatch

This is the same as the Power Snatch but uses one arm.

- This is a very demanding exercise and requires high levels of coordination and balance developed through significant practice.

- It's (highly) advisable that this lift is attempted only once the basics of the Power Snatch and DB Snatch have been mastered.

- Technique is as for the DB Snatch, with the dumbbell being replaced by a full Olympic bar.

SHOULDER STABILITY

All the lifts in this section focus on keeping the chest up, shoulderblades back and down at all times.

Plate Raise

- Hold a plate weight on the outside edges. Bend your knees slightly to absorb the weight.

- Keep your arms straight and your shoulderblades back and down. Lift the plate up to shoulder height. Don't lift with your shoulders or upper back to get the weight up.

- Hold and lower slowly and with control.

Stop Signs

■ Holding light dumbbells, stand with your elbows at right angles, pointing to the side.

■ Keep your upper arm parallel to the ground as you rotate your forearms up to a 90-degree angle so that they are vertical.

■ Lower back to the starting position.

Empty Can Raise

■ Holding light dumbbells, start with your arms hanging in front of your body.

■ Turn your arms in towards the centre of your body at about a 45-degree angle. Make sure your thumbs are pointing down towards the floor.

■ Raise your arms, maintaining the 45-degree turned-in arm position, until your hands are just above shoulder height.

■ Return to the starting position, reversing the arm movement.

TRAIN TOUGH

JUMPS FOR THE LOWER AND UPPER BODY

Squat Jump
- Stand with your weight balanced over both feet.

- In one quick movement, squat down and bounce up into a vertical jump, straightening your legs.

- Land evenly on both feet, and bend your knees to absorb the impact of the landing.

Split Jump
- Stand with your weight balanced over both feet. Shift one foot to sit in front of the other and redistribute your body weight.

- In one quick movement, squat down and bounce up into a vertical jump, driving up with the arms. Bend your knees up underneath you as far as you can.

- As you reach the top of the jump, switch the position of your feet so the other foot is in front.

- Land evenly on both feet (the opposite foot will be in front), and bend your knees to absorb the impact of the landing.

Lateral Jump

- Stand with your weight balanced over both feet.

- In one quick movement, squat down and jump to the right, as you move your legs apart.

- Land on your right foot, and bend your knee to absorb the impact of the landing.

- As soon as you land, push back to the left side, jumping up and landing on your left leg, and bend your knee to absorb the impact of the landing.

Single Leg Hitch

- Stand with your weight balanced over both feet.

- In one quick movement, squat down and bounce up into a vertical jump (drive hard with your arms).

- As you reach the top of the jump 'hitch' one heel up to your bum, quickly cycling it back down to prepare for the landing.

- Bend your knee on landing to absorb the impact.

TRAIN TOUGH

Borzov Jump

- Stand on one foot, raising the other leg behind you onto a bench or box.

- In one quick movement, squat down and bounce up into a vertical jump (drive hard with your arms).

- As you reach the top of the jump 'hitch' your heel up to your bum, quickly cycling it back down to prepare for the landing. Keep your other foot anchored to the bench or box behind you.

- Land on the same foot that you took off on, bending the knee to absorb the impact of the landing.

THIS JUMP IS NAMED AFTER THE GREAT RUSSIAN SPRINTER VALERIY BORZOV

Clap Push-ups

■ From a conventional push-up position, lower yourself to the ground, push up explosively and clap your hands once while in the air, then land back in the start position.

Depth Drop Push-ups

■ Set up two small boxes slightly further apart than the width of your shoulders.

■ Place your hands flat on top of the boxes and extend your legs out behind you in a push-up position.

■ Press up slightly and 'jump' off the boxes. Bring your hands underneath your chest, landing in a conventional push-up position. Bend your elbows to absorb the impact of the landing.

■ Immediately press back up into the air, moving your hands out so that they land in the original position on top of the boxes. Bend your elbows to absorb the impact of the landing.

TRAIN TOUGH

GENERAL PHYSICAL PREPARATION

Turkish Get Up
■ Lie flat on your back with your legs out straight and hip-width apart. Hold a dumbbell in one hand and raise the arm up vertically, keeping it straight.

■ Roll towards the 'weightless' arm and move to a sitting position. Extend your arm out behind you to prop your body up.

■ Slip the foot on the same side as the dumbbell up under your buttock, and push yourself into a deep squat position, while still holding the dumbbell up over your head.

■ Push up from the squat to a standing position with the dumbbell directly above the shoulder.

■ Reverse the movement, finishing back on the ground in your start position.

Burpees
■ Stand with your weight balanced over both feet.

■ Squat down to the ground and place both hands on the floor.

■ In one movement push your legs out straight behind you into a conventional push-up position (keep your back straight, don't sag in the middle).

■ Complete one push-up and push back into a standing position with your knees slightly bent and your hands on your hips.

■ Bounce up into a jump, then bend your knees to absorb the impact of the landing.

DB Squat and Reach

■ Stand with your weight balanced over both feet. In one hand hold a dumbbell. Bend the same leg as the arm holding the dumbbell up behind you at a right angle.

■ Pressing your weight down through your heel, squat down, keeping your bent leg at a 90-degree angle and then reach as far forward as possible with the hand holding the weight.

■ Touch the floor, then squeeze through the glutes and return to the start position, pushing the hips through as you straighten up.

■ Beginners should practise this exercise without the weight.

TRAIN TOUGH

Push-up variations

■ Start in a conventional push-up position, placing your hands about shoulder-width apart. Keep your shoulderblades back and down.

■ Lower your chest towards the ground.

■ Brace through the abs in order to maintain rigidity. Don't allow your mid-section to drop. Lower your chest, not your gut.

■ The hand position may be altered for variety (have a look at the pics).

Single Leg Bridge

■ Lie flat on the floor with one leg bent up at a 90-degree angle and the other leg stretched out along the floor. Place your hands behind your head.

■ Lift the straight leg so that it is in line with the thigh of the other leg.

■ Push the foot of the bent leg down and lift your hips off the ground, keeping both quads (thighs) parallel. Press your arms to the floor to anchor your body as you lift your hips.

GENERAL ADDITIONAL LIFTS

For the chest:
DB Incline Flys

■ Lie flat on an incline bench. Holding dumbbells, extend your arms up vertically above your chest, making sure your palms face towards each other.

■ Lower the dumbbells out to the side, keeping your arms as straight as possible, until they are parallel to the floor.

■ Bring your arms back to the starting position.

For the shoulders:
Military Press

■ Sit on a bench or stand on the floor with your feet shoulder-width apart.

■ Raise a barbell to your shoulders, keeping your chest high and your shoulderblades back and down, and your elbows in close to your body.

■ Press the bar to an arm's length overhead, using a slow and steady motion without swinging or arching your lower back. Bend your knees slightly to absorb some of the weight.

■ Lower slowly to the start position.

TRAIN TOUGH

Behind Neck Press
- Follow the instructions for the Military Press but the bar is placed behind your neck and is pushed from the shoulders.

DB Lateral Raise
- Stand in an upright position, placing one foot behind the other for balance.

- Hold dumbbells in front of your body and then raise them up to the side away from your body to a horizontal position. Keep arms just beyond a 90-degree angle.

Reverse DB Flys

■ Stand with your feet hip-width apart and your weight balanced over both feet.

■ Flex forward from the hips so that your torso is parallel to the floor.

■ Hold the dumbbells below your chest and keep your arms straight.

■ Raise your arms out to the side so that they are level with your body.

■ Reverse back to your start position.

Diesel Press

■ Stand with feet hip-width apart and your weight balanced over both feet.

■ Hold dumbbells down by your sides, then curl your arms up to the shoulders. Press up, raising the dumbbells above your shoulders and keeping your arms straight.

■ Reverse the movement back to the start position.

TRAIN TOUGH

Upright Row

- Stand with your chest up, and your shoulderblades back and down.

- Hold a bar in front of you with your hands spaced about 10–15 cm apart.

- Lift the bar up and over your chest, finishing the lift under your chin.

- Make sure your chest stays high and don't drop your body forward, as you return the bar to the start position.

For the Upper Back (Lats and rhomboids):

Seated Row

- Sitting on a rowing machine, hold your chest up and keep your shoulderblades back and down. Keep your abdominal muscles tight.

- Flex forward from the hip, and pull the weight back towards your chest. Draw your elbows back and keep them close to your body, pulling the weight toward the chest.

- Stop as soon as your elbow joints are in line with your shoulders. Reverse the motion and return to the start position.

Rope Row

- Hold your chest up and keep your shoulderblades back and down throughout the exercise. Keep your abdominal muscles tight. Stand tall and place one foot behind you to anchor your balance.

- Using ropes connected to a cable pulley, grab the ropes and pull, drawing your elbows back past your ribs. As you pull the ropes towards you, squeeze your shoulderblades together. Make sure your elbows stay close to your body.

- Bend your knees slightly to adjust to the tension of the cable.

- Under control, reverse the motion and slowly return to the start position.

Close Grip Overhand Row

- Hold your chest up and keep your shoulderblades back and down throughout the exercise. Keep your abdominal muscles tight. Stand tall and place one foot behind you to anchor your balance.

- This exercise may be done seated or standing, using a short bar connected to a cable pulley.

- Grip the bar using an overhand technique. and pull, drawing your elbows back past your ribs. As you pull the cable towards you, squeeze your shoulderblades together. Make sure your elbows stay close to your body.

- Bend your knees slightly to adjust to the tension of the cable.

- Under control, reverse the motion and slowly return to the start position.

TRAIN TOUGH

Close Grip Underhand Row

■ Same exercise as the Overhand Row but use an underhand grip.

TRAINING TIPS

■ All rowing movements employ the same skill set to execute each exercise.

■ Using the standing version of the above lifts ultimately limits the amount of weight that can be lifted. Using the same technical components in a pulldown machine allows you to lift greater weight.

Pulldowns

■ You do these using a Pulldown machine that can usually be found in most gyms.

■ Grips may be varied as for Chin-ups.

For the trapezius (the muscles running from the base of the ear out to the shoulder and down to the middle of the back):

DB Shrug

■ Stand tall with your chest up and your shoulderblades back and down.

■ Holding dumbbells by your side, 'shrug' your shoulders up towards your ears. Hold briefly and then lower to the start position.

Run the Rack

■ This torturous variation can be applied to almost any dumbbell exercise but was made for DB Shrugs.

■ Select the heaviest dumbbell you can handle for the first prescribed set.

■ Once you have finished, take the next set of dumbbells down and complete the next set.

■ Continue 'running the rack' until the set is finished, or you fall over.

Snatch (Wide) Grip Shrug
■ Stand with your feet shoulder-width apart.

■ Grasp the bar in a wide snatch grip.

■ Keep the arms straight and 'shrug' your shoulders up towards your ears.

For the triceps:
Lying Triceps Extensions
(Skull Crushers)
These can be done using a variety of benches (incline, decline, flat) and are good for extra triceps work.

■ Lie on your back on a bench with a bar held at arm's length above your shoulders.

■ Lower the bar in a semi-circular motion, bending your arms at the elbows. Keep your upper arms vertical until your forearms touch your biceps.

■ Return to the start position and repeat.

TRAIN TOUGH

Overhead Cable Tricep Extension

- Face away from a low pulley. Hands are held above the head with the cable behind.

- Elbows are bent to lower the weight (only the forearms move) and extended back to the start to complete the movement.

For the biceps:
Standard Arm Curl

- Stand tall with your shoulderblades held back and down. With an underhand grip, hold a bar at arm's length in front of your thighs, with your palms facing out. (This exercise can also be done with dumbbells.)

- Raise your forearms and bring the bar up as far as you can, making sure that your hands and wrists stay vertically aligned with the elbows in the top position.

- Return the bar to the start position to finish.

TB Curl

- Lie on a therapeutic ball with your torso at approximately 45-degrees. Balance by using your knees as an anchor.

- Extend your arms over the ball holding either a bar or dumbbells. Your forearms and palms should face outwards.

- Hold your chest up, and flex at the elbows to bring the bar up towards you.

- Make sure your hands remain in front of the elbows in the top position.

- Return to the start position to finish.

Cable Curl
- Grasp a low pulley cable bar with a shoulder-width underhand grip.

- Stand close to the pulley.

- With the elbows to the side, raise the bar until the forearms are vertical.

- Lower until the arms are fully extended.

- Changing the height of the cable will alter the exercise and add variety.

DB Hammer Curl
- Stand tall with your shoulderblades held back and down. Hold a dumbbell by your side using an overhand grip. Your palms will be facing in to your body.

- Lift your forearms and curl the dumb-bell up towards your biceps. Keep your hands firm and your palms facing inwards.

- Reverse the curl movement back to the start position.

Matrix Curls
- Matrix drills are a whole training entity in their own right. Matrix Curls are sometimes referred to as 'sevens' and can be used with any of the curl variations described.

- From the start position curl up to halfway for 7 reps.

- From half-way curl up to the top position for a further 7 reps.

- Finish with 7 full reps.

Reverse Curls
These use the same technique as Standard Curls except you hold the bar with an overhand grip.

TRAIN TOUGH

For the legs:
Leg Press
- These are done on the Leg Press machine, which is a standard piece of equipment in most gyms.

- Keep feet approximately shoulder-width apart, with toes aligned along top of plate.

- Lower the weight down until the knees are at approximately 90-degrees.

- Press down through the heels to return the weight to the start position.

Leg Curl
- The Leg Curl machine is another standard piece of equipment.

- May be in a lying, kneeling, seated or standing position.

- Always keep hip fixed when using this equipment. Avoid swinging the hips to gain momentum in order to lift the weight especially in the standing position.

Single Leg Calf Raise
- Place one foot on the edge of a small elevated platform or step. Bend the other leg and hold it up.

- Stand tall, keeping hips and shoulders square. Lower the heel down over the edge of the platform or step, then press back up onto the toes.

FOUNDATION TRAINING

8 BUILDING THE BLOCKS

Talk to any builder and they'll tell you that solid foundations are vital. This applies equally to the strength and conditioning field. You can't go to the gym and lift heavy or get out on the track and sprint like a madman without a solid platform. The platform in this case is the region between your bottom ribs and the top of your hips – and don't forget, the ribs go all the way around the back.

The foundation muscles include:

- **Transversus abdominis:** the deep circular muscle that surrounds your guts. When contracted, this muscle draws the belly button in, increasing intra-abdominal pressure and protects the spine.

- **Obliques:** the angulated muscles that run from the ribs to the top of the hips and generate rotational and lateral bending (flexion) movement.

- **Rectus abdominis:** the muscles that run from the front of the ribs down to the lower part of the pelvis just above the pubic region. These muscles are responsible for bending (flexing) movements.

- **Erector spinae:** the thick group of muscles either side of your spine running from the lower back up to the ribs. These muscles are responsible for straightening the body when it is in a bent position.

To build a powerful foundation, it's critical that all of the above-mentioned muscles are given balanced training loads. Forcing one muscle group too much leads to the neglect of the others. This creates an unbalanced and functionally poor foundation.

This form of neglect is seen all too often in local gyms as people overwork the rectus abdominis muscles in pursuit of the much sought-after six-pack. The funny thing is that many men with a visibly appealing stomach are often some of the weakest when it comes to foundation strength. Indeed the washboard look is more a function of good diet and genetics. Irrespective of appearance, powerful foundation muscles are the cornerstone to reaching more advanced training techniques – and results.

CHEAT NOTES

An easy way to understand intra-abdominal pressure is to think of a new tube of toothpaste. You can poke the tube and it feels reasonably soft (like many people's mid-sections). If you place your hand around the tube and squeeze (with a bit of force) you will get to a point where the tube feels quite solid. This is because your hand has applied pressure to the toothpaste forcing it to move up and down (away from the pressure) where it meets resistance from the lid and the base of the tube. At this point the toothpaste has nowhere to go and cannot be compressed any further. This increases the pressure within the tube proportionally to the amount of force applied by your hand. Now apply this idea to your abdominal cavity. Force applied by the transverse abdominis increases the pressure within the cavity, which then provides a greater degree of support for the spine. Remember, only with a moderate amount of force, not a maximum amount of force. Research has shown that full-on voluntary contraction of the abdominals reduces transverse abdominis activity.

SUCK IT UP

SUCK IT UP

Do you ever get a tight lower back sitting all day at the office or in the driver's seat? The first step toward a solid platform is getting the deep foundation muscles working. Posture plays a large part in this. Improving your posture can be done with practice and feedback (either from a friend or a coach, or looking at your posture in the mirror). The endurance capacity of the muscles that support posture can also be improved by regular use of posture related drills. Remember the aim of the game with improving posture is to make it a natural position to maintain, not a forced one. Try the following drills several times a day. Your back will thank you.

■ When sitting or standing try holding your shoulderblades slightly back, and down. Your chest should be lifted up (imagine being pulled up by your sternum).
  • Gently draw your belly button in towards your spine. The deep muscles don't function well when stimulated to their maximum point. These muscles are built for endurance and are stability muscles, which means they respond to light contractions over a long period.

  • Your breathing should be natural and rhythmic, not forced or restricted. As you breathe out, gently draw your pelvic floor up (imagine trying to stop urine flow). This stimulates the deep musculature at the front and back of the abdominal cavity. Macho guys might think only women should work these muscles, but I've seen Anna-Louise Bouvier, a physiotherapist and author of *Fix Your Back* (ABC Books), use this method to fix pretty significant injuries in international rugby players.

TRAIN TOUGH

Once you've got a handle on these basics try using them for these exercises.

■ **Prone support knees:** Hold the postural positions described above while supporting your body on your elbows and knees.

Variations:
- On elbows and knees
- On hands with feet on a therapeutic ball (TB) ball
- Elbows and knees with load placed on the hips.

■ **Lateral support:**
Complete as for the Prone support exercise but do this from the side. It is critical to maintain and focus on the 'chest up' position as the natural tendency will be to collapse forward.

Variation Static Star
- Hold the position as above adding the top arm fully extended and the top leg lifted until parallel to the ground.

To make the whole package work efficiently these basic posture skills need to be transferred to all other methods of training. It's not hard, but you do have to think about it.

THE SIX PACK — SOMETHING A LITTLE DIFFERENT!

Hanging abs

Hanging ab exercises (such as raising your knees while hanging on the chin-up bar) are fantastic for developing core strength. They include movement of the spine and hips, linking the abdominal and hip flexor musculature. They're also fantastic for helping with improving your speed (given hips and abs work together in driving the knee forward at high velocity).

Hanging Knee Raise

Hang with legs straight, where bar allows. Without swinging the body lift the knees up toward chin height and lower under control. A big portion of this exercise is learning to control the swing.

Hanging Lateral Knee Raise

As for Hanging Knee Raise, except the knees are brought up laterally so that the top shin finishes approximately parallel to the ground. Return to start under control.

NEWS FLASH

You don't have to lie on your back to train the big abdominal muscles. Lying on your back and completing endless low-intensity crunches does little to help improve the movement in these muscles. Use a variety of positions to help you strengthen your abdominal musculature in as many planes of movement as possible.

TB crunches (using full range)

Lie with the ball positioned in the small of the back. Feet must be secured to the ground by either a weight or partner. The lower body must remain fixed at all times. Start the movement fully extended, that is, lying right back on the ball so that your back conforms to the curve of the ball.

NB: The idea is not to go so far back that you experience any discomfort. Allow yourself to go far back enough that with the addition of a deep breath you can feel your abs stretch. The upper body is lifted by flexing the trunk, not by lifting from the hips. Do not allow hips to roll down the ball to assist in lifting the upper body – they must remain fixed. The top position is achieved when the ribs are as close to the hips as possible.

Variations:

- Start with your arms crossed on chest
- Fold your arms behind head
- Extend your arms straight above the head
- Add a dumbbell to your chest keeping it high on the collarbones at all times

The benefit of the therapeutic ball in this exercise compared to the exercises done on the floor is that the abdominal muscles get stretched to their full potential. On the floor, the muscles are not worked through their full range of motion, which means they receiving limited stimulus and therefore will be limited in their performance potential.

TRAINING TIP

The key to successfully achieving the top position is not to allow the shoulders to pass over the hips. Once this occurs the leverage system employed to make abs work will be altered sufficiently that the exercise becomes ineffective.

Jacknife

Just for old times sake, one of the classics.

■ Lie on the floor with your back flat. Keep your legs straight.

■ Extend both arms above your head.

■ Under control and pivoting on the hip, bring hands and feet together at the top of the movement. Return under control to the ground. If you are sadistic try them loaded with a medicine ball between the feet and a light dumbbell in your hands

TRAIN TOUGH

TURN AND BURN

One of the most neglected spinal movements is rotation. Imagine a line extending from the top of your head down through your pelvis – a vertical skewer, if you like. Rotation involves movement around that line. Rotational exercises can be done in a variety of positions and with a variety of equipment. There should be no excuse for neglecting this type of exercise.

A GREAT ROTATIONAL TRAINING RULE IS: HONKER, HANDS, HEART

Keep your HONKER (nose), HANDS, and HEART (sternum) aligned. For those who don't get it, stand straight, lock your arms and lift them until they are parallel to the ground and clasp your hands together. Look straight down your nose and you will see that your nose, sternum and hands are all aligned. When doing rotational exercises stick to this alignment all the time. While standing rotate as far as you can to the left without breaking this alignment. Do the same to the right. This range of movement is as far as you need to go in order to effectively work your rotational musculature. Going further will break the alignment, and you will end up using your shoulder joints to get more rotation, which is not what we are trying to work on here. Be disciplined and hold the position. You will reap the rewards.

Cable Woodchop

- Stand next to to a high cable pulley with your feet wider than shoulder width.

- Grasp the handle with the outside hand first, then lock the upper body as described above. Rotate toward the pulley maintaining the upper body position.

Cable Rip

■ Set yourself up as for the Cable Woodchop above.

During the execution of the lift the difference is that as your body comes around the shoulder is dropped onto the cable and the movement is continued to the limit of range of movement. The shorter lever allows more resistance to be used, thereby making this exercise quite a bit more aggressive than the Cable Woodchop. Ensure it is executed with the correct attitude or you will be humbled!

TRAINING TIP

If you get all the way round to face the pulley check your technique or join the circus, because you have exceeded the functional rotational capacity of your spine. The rotation movement should occur through the abdominal region (lumbar spine) only. Allowing the arms to drift across the body, that is, not maintaining the 'Hands and Heart' section of the mantra, utilises the shoulders and will not contribute to rotational strength.

To lift the weight, maintain the upper body position and rotate down at approximately 45°, sweeping the cable around using the abs to generate the movement. As you become more proficient you can release the hip slightly so that the hips and abs work in synchronicity to lift the load.

TRAIN TOUGH

Plate Woodchop

As with the Cable Rip, this exercise is a far more dynamic and aggressive version of the Cable Woodchop. Setup is as for the Cable version; however, instead of gripping a cable, grip a plate. The principles of the movement are the same as the Cable version but the hips are given more freedom to move as this exercise is aimed at developing 'system strength' which refers to the ability of a group of muscles moving in sequence to generate force.

NB: Make sure you master the Cable Woodchop before progressing to this version, and when you do, start with a light weight and slowly until you get the movement pattern correct. Use a mirror for technique reinforcement.

P.S. Don't forget to complete the exercise on both sides!

Phew... that was real!

TRAINING TIP

Because this exercise is not bound to conform to the pattern of movement as dictated by a cable pulley, it is critical that the plate is accelerated vigorously in both directions. The easiest way to achieve this is to establish the end points for the movement before you start, ie simply go through the movement without a weight and figure out the start and the finish. With the addition of the plate picture the end points in your mind's eye. The objective then is to accelerate the plate as fast as possible to the end point at the top of the range, brake the weight as it arrives at the end point and then accelerate it aggressively back toward the lower end point, again braking it HARD and reversing the load. Accelerating, braking and reaccelerating the load in the opposite direction places immense stress on the rotational musculature.

Round the World

- Stand with feet wider than shoulder width, with a plate gripped in front at approximately hip height.

- Imagine a circular track extending from the plate, up over your right shoulder (clearing it by approximately 20 – 30 cm), continuing smoothly over your head, down over the left shoulder (clearing it by approximately 20 – 30 cm) back to the start. This is the path the plate will follow.

- Start at the bottom, swing the plate up over the right shoulder, bring it smoothly over the head, and down the left side stopping it at the start position, reversing it and retracing the track back over the shoulders and head going left to right. Completing both sides constitutes one rep.

TRAINING TIP

As for the Plate Woodchop make sure you get the basics in place before trying this, and when you do start slow and light!

Medicine Ball Juggle

This is one of the most dynamic abdominal exercises you will ever try! You want to be well advanced in all the preceding exercises before attempting this one.

■ Stand with feet wider than shoulder width with a medicine ball in both hands.

■ Start by throwing one ball up into the air (this is the hard bit as you only use one arm).

The aim is to have the balls track vertically just outside the width of your shoulders so that you have to rotate your torso to get to the next ball. As the first ball begins to fall (and this will be quicker than you think), get the other ball up in the air, ensuring that you throw it as straight as possible so that it will be in the right place when you get back. Repeat the process on both sides for desired time or rep range.

GET MOVING OR YOU WILL BE CHASING MEDICINE BALLS ALL OVER THE PLACE!

Loaded Half Pepper Grinder and Loaded Pepper Grinder

Both these exercises are executed with the same core techniques.

■ Lie flat on your back with both arms extended at a 90-degree angle to the body. In the Half version knees are bent, while in the full version the legs are straight.

■ A medicine ball placed at the knees (half) or the feet (full) provide extra resistance for suitable individuals. Brace the upper body and rotate the legs to the ground attempting to maintain a 90-degree angle between the legs and body. Rotate from one side to the other for the desired reps.

TRAIN TOUGH

LOAD UP, LOAD UP...

One of the things limiting many guys' development is that their abdominal exercises are done at low to non-existent intensity, with massive reps that leave them so bored they give up. Most of the exercises in this section can be overloaded using medicine balls, plates or stacks of weights. The key with overloading abdominal exercises is to *start out slowly*. There's nothing to gain from attempting large resistance from the outset. Exercises must *always* be completed with perfect technique. Technique must never be compromised in order to load more weight.

Lateral Flexion is one of the most overlooked abdominal movements, and one that can be effectively trained using external resistance.

Dumbbell Laterals

■ Stand with feet wider than shoulder width apart, dumbbell in one hand, and opposite hand on the side of the head.

■ Locking the hips in place, simply flex (bend) laterally (sideways) ensuring that you do not move forward or backward, just sideways. The movement is quite small and should be executed in front of a mirror to monitor exercise technique. The hand holding the weight should reach approximately the level of the knee.

■ On the way back to the start, focus on pulling the load up using the abdominals on contralateral (opposite) side.

Olympic Bar Laterals

Technically the same lift as described above for the DB version. The exception is that the Olympic bar provides a challenge to hold and considerably greater resistance.

Lying Lateral Raise

This version of lateral flexion utilises gravity as the resistance.

■ Lie on your side on a flat bench with your hip on the edge of the bench and have a training partner hold you at the knee and ankle.

■ Keep your chest up and the shoulderblades back and down, and lower yourself approximately 30 – 40 cm (remember the range of movement in this exercise is not big). Focus on lifting from the lateral abdominal region and raise the torso up just above horizontal and return to the start.

MAINTAIN THE CORRECT POSTURAL ALIGNMENT (SUCK IT UP) AT ALL TIMES.

Dragon Slayer (I pinched this from someone but can't remember who ... so if you read this, thanks!)

This takes the Lying Lateral Raise and adds in some rotation to create an extremely challenging exercise.

- Set up as for the Lying Lateral Raise. Add a light medicine ball (don't attempt this with a metal weight) aligned as described for Cable Woodchop (Honker, Hands, Heart – see p 102).

- Hold your torso in the horizontal position. Rotate down to lower the ball, then rotate up releasing the ball at the top of the movement. As the ball returns, decelerate it as you rotate back down.

- Continue for desired reps, then repeat on the other side.

TRAINING TIPS

- Beginners may find it more productive to start with their legs bent.
- Don't swing the arm as this will only add momentum to the movement, which will reduce the work done by the abs.

Lateral Jacknife

Simple old school exercise that can be implemented effectively anywhere.

- Lie on your side with the top arm over your head and the bottom arm bracing on the floor at 90-degrees. Keep the feet together and simultaneously raise the legs and the top arm bringing them together at the top of the movement.

Loaded Lateral Jacknife

Same as above, just harder. Hold a dumbbell in your top hand and have a small medicine ball between your legs. The key here is not to throw the weight up but rather to lift under control.

STRAIGHTEN UP, YOUNG MAN

The erector spinae (ES) muscles run up your back from the pelvis to approximately the level of your shoulderblades. Erector spinae actually describes a group of muscles including important little ones like the multifidus, which cause the extension of the spine or the straightening of the body from a bent position.

The ES muscles are trained regularly during exercises such as the Good Morning, Romanian Deadlift and the conventional Deadlift. They can also be trained specifically using variations of the Deadlift detailed in Chapter 7, 'Strength exercises'.

TRAIN TOUGH

THE PROGRAMS
Looking to put it all together? These killer programs will help to reshape that gut in no time.

Beginner Cycle
Alternate programs I & II 2 to 3 times per week, eg Monday B I, Tuesday B II, Thursday B I etc.

B I

EXERCISE	NOTES	WEEK 1	WEEK 2	WEEK 3	WEEK 4
Prone Support Knees		3 x 30 sec	3 x 40 sec	3 x 50 sec	3 x 60 sec
Prone Support Knees		3 x 30 sec	3 x 40 sec	2 x 50 sec	2 x 60 sec
Hanging Single Knee Raise	Same technique as for two legs – just use one!	3 x 5 each side	3 x 7 each side	3 x 10 each side	2 x 10 each side
TB Crunch	No additional load	4 x 6	4 x 8	2 x 10	2 x 10
DB Laterals	Prescribed loads may be increased to a max of 10kg.	3 x 10 @ 5 kg	3 x 12 @ 5 kg	3 x 10 @ 7.5 kg	3 x 12 @ 7.5 kg
Lateral Jacknife	No extra load. Start with knees bent	3 x 8 each side	3 x 10 each side	3 x 6 each side, legs straight	3 x 8 each side, legs straight

B II

EXERCISE	NOTES	WEEK 1	WEEK 2	WEEK 3	WEEK 4
Lateral Support	Reps completed on each side	3 x 30 sec	3 x 40 sec	2 x 50 sec	2 x 60 sec
Half Pepper Grinder	BW only, no extra load	2 x 8 each side	2 x 10 each side	2 x 12 each side	2 x 14 each side
Cable Woodchop	Use light load only	3 x 10 each side	3 x 12 each side (use same load as week 1)	3 x 10 each side (increase load from previous week)	3 x 12 each side (use same load as week 3)
Jacknife		2 x 6	2 x 8	3 x 6	3 x 8
DB Laterals	Use light load only	3 x 10 each side	3 x 12 each side (use same load as week 1)	3 x 10 each side (increase load from previous week)	3 x 12 each side (use same load as week 3)

INTERMEDIATE CYCLE

Alternate programs I & II 2 to 3 times per week, eg Monday Inter I, Tuesday Inter II, Thursday Inter I etc.

Inter I

EXERCISE	NOTES	WEEK 1	WEEK 2	WEEK 3	WEEK 4
Prone Support		2 x 45 sec	2 x 60 sec	3 x 45 sec	3 x 60 sec
Hanging Knee Raise	Controlled pace, strict technique	3 x 6	3 x 8	3 x 10	2 x 12
TB Crunch Loaded	Increase load, maintaining strict technique	3 x 8	3 x 10 (use same load as week 1)	3 x 8 (increase load from week 2)	3 x 10 (use same load as week 3)
DB Laterals	Increase load, maintaining strict technique	3 x 8	3 x 10 (use same load as week 1)	3 x 8 (increase load from week 2)	3 x 10 (use same load as week 3)
Lateral Jacknife	Use full position	2 x 8 each side	2 x 10 each side	2 x 12 each side	1 x 12 each side

Inter II

EXERCISE	NOTES	WEEK 1	WEEK 2	WEEK 3	WEEK 4
Lateral Support	Full position	2 x 45 sec each side	2 x 60 sec each side	3 x 45 sec each side	3 x 60 sec each side
Pepper Grinder	Full position	2 x 8 each side	2 x 10 each side	2 x 12 each side	1 x 12 each side
Cable Woodchop	Increase load, maintain strict technique	3 x 8	3 x 10 (use same load as week 1)	3 x 8 (increase load from week 2)	3 x 10 (use same load as week 3)
Jacknife	Full position	2 x 6	2 x 8	2 x 10	2 x 10
Lying Lateral Raise	Full position	2 x 4 each side	2 x 6 each side	2 x 8 each side	2 x 10 each side

TRAIN TOUGH

ADVANCED CYCLE

Alternate programs I & II 2 to 3 times per week, eg Monday A I, Tuesday A II, Thursday A I etc.

A I

EXERCISE	NOTES	WEEK 1	WEEK 2	WEEK 3	WEEK 4
Prone Support	Place moderate load on back of pelvis (not to exceed 20 kg)	2 x 45 sec	2 x 60 sec (same load as week 1)	2 x 45 sec (increase load from week 2)	2 x 60 sec (same load as week 3)
Hanging Knee Raise	Add load via med-ball between knees. Stay strict.	2 x 6 (approx 2 kg ball)	2 x 8 (approx 2 kg ball)	2 x 6 (approx 4 kg ball)	2 x 8 (approx 4 kg ball)
TB Crunch Loaded	Increase load – maintaining strict technique	3 x 8	3 x 10 (use same load as week 1)	3 x 8 (increase load from week 2)	3 x 10 (use same load as week 3)
Olympic Bar Laterals	Increase load – maintaining strict technique	2 x 8	2 x 10 (use same load as week 1)	2 x 8 (increase load from week 2)	2 x 10 (use same load as week 3).
Cable Rip	Increase load – maintaining strict technique	2 x 8	2 x 10 (use same load as week 1)	2 x 8 (increase load from week 2)	2 x 10 (use same load as week 3)

A II

EXERCISE	NOTES	WEEK 1	WEEK 2	WEEK 3	WEEK 4
Static Star	Full position	2 x 45 sec each side	2 x 60 sec each side	3 x 45 sec each side	3 x 60 sec each side
Loaded Pepper Grinder	Increase load, maintaining strict technique	2 x 8	2 x 10 (use same load as week 1)	2 x 8 (increase load from week 2)	2 x 10 (use same load as week 3)
Plate Woodchop	Start slow and light	2 x 8 each side	2 x 10 each side (use same load as week 1)	2 x 8 each side (increase load from week 2)	2 x 10 each side (use same load as week 3)
Loaded Jacknife	Increase load, maintaining strict technique	2 x 8 each side	2 x 10 each side (use same load as week 1)	2 x 8 each side (increase load from week 2)	2 x 10 each side (use same load as week 3)
Loaded Lying Lateral Raise	Increase load, maintaining strict technique	2 x 8 each side	2 x 10 each side (use same load as week 1)	2 x 8 each side (increase load from week 2)	2 x 10 each side (use same load as week 3)

PS:
If you have successfully completed all of the preceding work, it is truly time to crank it up a notch. There is an additional Extreme Cycle that you can use once per week in conjunction with the Advanced Cycle. Get the low-down in the 'Sealed Section' on p 209.

FUSION TRAINING
9 STRENGTH AND CONDITIONING IN ONE LIFT

Fusion training is by no means a new concept nor is it something I claim to have invented. It's just a name I've put to a style of circuit training involving both strength and conditioning in a single session.

Now, without doubt, strength and fitness purists will be up in arms, asserting that the combination of two opposed training methods detracts from the specificity of the session. (Strictly speaking sessions should be restricted to training specific elements of physical performance – using strength and fitness means in the one session may be considered inefficient for a competitive athlete, but for the time-restricted recreational athlete this approach can be very effective.)

Well, technically I agree. But in this type of session you aren't aiming to develop, improve or expand your ability to lift heavier or run longer. The aim of fusion training is to tolerate more work across a broad spectrum of means.

Fusion training comes from the work of athletes in sports such as rowing (still water and surf), wrestling (including Ultimate Fighting), and some old school training techniques from rugby.

Very simply: fusion training combines interval-based fitness with hypertrophy/strength/endurance training. While the concept appears easy, the execution is a world away from anything most people have done before. The biggest challenge is to tolerate the physiological variation.

For instance:

■ When you lie down to do an exercise like a bench press, your blood pressure drops (stands to reason – you no longer have to pump blood uphill). When you do hard interval training your blood pressure rises (along with your heart rate) to support the extra need for oxygen in the muscles. Try doing these two back-to-back and see how you handle variations in blood pressure. (Careful, don't faint!)

■ Strength training when done to fatigue (usually with reps more than 8–10) produces a large amount of waste in the blood which must be removed. This is done by converting some of those products to carbon dioxide and breathing them out (ever noticed how you get quite puffed doing higher reps?). Now, imagine putting yourself in this state then jumping on a treadmill for a couple of 3 min efforts at 80 per cent MHR. Feel the burn, as they say, with the added demand on your lungs and circulatory system.

Fusion training suits the recreational athlete with an established background in strength and fitness training. It's not the ideal session to go out and try on your first visit to the gym. It needs to be left to those with a solid fitness base. But why would anybody want to subject themselves to a fusion training session? Good question!

One of the benefits is the variety. Unlike competitive athletes who need to train with the highest degree of specificity at all times, the recreational athlete is not bound by limits. Sessions of varied means can be used in a variety of combinations, for no other reason than just for something different. For most people, the gym, even the outdoor workout, can get a bit monotonous. Even with all the planning and goal setting in the world the human heart wants to venture into the unknown. Fusion training sessions are fantastic because they not only provide a physical challenge, they also pose a mental one – the variety places a greater demand on the mind to drive the body forward. This is why you need to have your body in gear before you have a real crack.

On the purely physical front, the benefits of this type of training are numerous:

- Strength training in a session promotes the release of powerful hormones (growth hormone, testosterone, and so on) that use fat, therefore reducing body fat levels.

- Strength endurance training, although not the most efficient at generating muscle mass, will spark growth when completed at a maximal intensity (that is, to failure).

- The use of interval-based locomotor (running, riding, paddling) or ergonomically based training (rowing machine, treadmill) contributes to the development and maintenance of a strong cardiovascular system.

- Because of the extreme nature of fusion training, a very high level of energy is expended during every session. This, again, burns body fat.

FUSION TRAINING COMBINES INTERVAL-BASED FITNESS WITH HYPERTROPHY/ STRENGTH/ ENDURANCE TRAINING.

TRAIN TOUGH

STRENGTH TRAINING AND FUSION TRAINING SESSIONS

Like any session involving strength elements, a few details need to be established before getting started:

■ What weight to lift.

■ How many times to lift it.

Guidelines for establishing the strength components of your fusion training session are:

■ Primarily use exercises that utilise big muscle groups – squats, deadlift, bench press – as these require greater energy than those involving small muscles. This will increase the total energy cost for the session.

■ Small musculature exercises – bicep curls, lateral dumbbell raises – while not as energy demanding as the bigger exercises, still provide a significant pump to the muscle if worked hard.

■ Don't attempt to use maximal loads during a fusion session! Because the level of fatigue will be greater the longer the session goes, your ability to exert the necessary force to move maximum or near-maximum loads will be reduced. Leave maximum strength training to a separate part of your program.

■ Technique must never be compromised. If you find your technique failing, reduce the load. Retain the same reps but complete them with lighter resistance.

FITNESS TRAINING AND FUSION TRAINING SESSIONS

Guidelines for establishing the fitness components of your fusion training session are:

■ Interval training techniques are best suited to fusion training sessions. Long slow distance (LSD) training requires a separate session.

■ Interval length should be no longer than about 4 min. The aim of the session is to provide variety. Intervals that go too long stall the flow of the session.

■ It's best suited to individuals who already have a solid base of aerobic conditioning and can benefit from short, sharp intensity-based intervals.

■ Exercise modes requiring the carrying of body weight (such as running) and those using upper- and lower-body activity simultaneously will generate the greatest energy demand, stimulating metabolic rate and burning fat.

■ Either locomotor (running, riding, paddling) or cross-training (XTR) modes can be used. The most effective and accessible are listed opposite.

MODE	POSITIVES	NEGATIVES
Running	Ideally done outdoors, may use treadmill. High level of energy expenditure.	Easier to get lower limb soreness due to high impact.
Bike	Usually lots of stationary bikes in gyms.	Logistically tough to use in a fusion training session. Must lower heart rate (HR) goals by approximately 5 bpm.
Orbit walker with arm action	Very demanding piece of equipment. Very high energy expenditure (this is lower on machine without arm action). Non-impact activity – limited soreness.	May tighten hip flexors to some extent.
Rowing machine or ergometer ('erg' for short)	Very demanding piece of equipment. Very high energy expenditure. With a strong back and good technique, soreness is minimal.	Equipment without a 'floating head' may cause back soreness. Electronic-based rowing machines are a waste of time. Moderate level of skill required to be efficient.
Skipping	Highly demanding when done at pace. Excellent coordination drill.	High level of skill required.
Boxing	Very demanding when completed aggressively. Limited soreness (after your hands get used to it).	Moderate level of skill required for efficient use. Some risk of injury to hands – particularly for over-zealous beginners.
Arm grinder	Very demanding when completed aggressively. No soreness due to lack of impact.	Must lower heart rate (HR) goals by approximately 5 bpm. May fatigue quickly due to use of small muscle mass.

TRAIN TOUGH

Beginner

ORDER	EXERCISE	CONTENT	TIME
A	Bike / Treadmill / Orbit walker	2 x 3 min @ Zone 3 with 1 min recovery	8 min
B1	Push Ups	2 x 10 with 30 sec recovery	5 min
B2	UG chin-ups	2 x 8 with 30 sec recovery	5 min
C	Bike / Treadmill / Orbit walker	2 x 3 min @ Zone 3 with 1 min recovery	8 min
D1	Split Squat (no weight)	2 x 12 each leg	5 min
D2	Burpees	2 x 10	5 min
E	Bike / Treadmill / Orbit walker	2 x 3 min @ Zone 3 with 1 min recovery	8 min
F	CORE Circuit	Back Extensions 2 x 10 Cable Woodchop 2 x 10 each side Old School Sit Up 2 x 10	5 min
TOTAL TIME			39 min

Intermediate

ORDER	EXERCISE	CONTENT	TIME
A	Rowing Erg	2 x 2 min >550 m, 1 min between sets	6 min
B	Strength Set	Squat 1 x 12 – no recovery Military Press 1 x 12 – 90 sec recovery	3.5 min
C	Rowing Erg	2 x 2 min >570 m, 1 min between sets	6 min
D	Strength Set	Deadlift 1 x 12 – no recovery Bench Press 1 x 12 – 90 sec recovery	3.5 min
E	Rowing Erg	2 x 2 min >590 m, 1 min between sets	6 min
F	Strength Set	Split Squat 1 x 12 – no recovery Diesel Press 1 x 12 – 90 sec recovery	3.5 min
TOTAL TIME			37.5 min

Advanced

ORDER	EXERCISE	CONTENT	TIME
A	Run or XTR	3 min @ Zone 3 – 30 sec recovery 2 min @ Zone 3 – 30 sec recovery 1 min @ Zone 4 – 2 min recovery	9 min
B	Strength Set	Bench Press 2 x 10 – no recovery Chin-ups (UG) 2 x 10 – 90 sec recovery	5 min
C	Run or XTR	1 min @ Zone 4 – 30 sec recovery 2 min @ Zone 3 – 30 sec recovery 3 min @ Zone 3 – 2 min recovery	9 min
D	Strength Set	Squat 2 x 10 – no recovery Back Extensions 2 x 10 – 90 sec recovery	5 min
E	Run or XTR	3 min @ Zone 3 – 30 sec recovery 2 min @ Zone 3 – 30 sec recovery 1 min @ Zone 4 – 2 min recovery	9 min
F	Strength Set	Dips 2 x 10 – no recovery Diesel Press 2 x 10 – 90 sec recovery	5 min
G	CORE Circuit	Hanging Knee Raise 2 x 10 Loaded Russian Twist 2 x 10 Loaded TB Crunch 2 x 10	10 min
TOTAL TIME			52 min

TRAIN TOUGH

Challenge session

I call this 'the Dribbler', so named after an international rugby player who dribbles profusely everytime he does this session.

NB: Treadmill, rowing erg or orbit walker with arms only to be used.

May also be completed outside using running.

ORDER	EXERCISE	CONTENT	TIME
A	Run or XTR	2 x 2 min HR Zone 4 – 1 min recovery between sets	6 min
B	20 kg Bar Circuit	10 reps of each: Upright Row Shoulder Press Behind Neck Press Standing Jerk Press (power clean bar to chest then press) Curls Completed continuously for 2 min –1 min recovery	3 min
		Repeat A and B, 3 x total	
The Finale	Rowing erg	Substitute 2 min 600 m	6 min

GUIDELINES FOR INCORPORATING FUSION SESSIONS INTO YOUR PROGRAM

So now you've had a look at a couple of fusion training sessions (you might have even had a go at one), you need to think about where this type of training fits into your overall plan. Here are some guidelines to help you introduce this very aggressive form of training into your program. And the abbreviations to help you out here are strength training (STR), fitness training (FIT), fusion training session (FTS).

TRAINING TIP

Separate the STR and FTS sessions with the greatest number of days. Residual fatigue from STR will have greater impact on FTS than will fatigue from FIT. Dig?

Introduce a session during the last week of a cycle for a real pick-up in intensity:

- Week 1–3: Mon: STR
  - Tue: FIT
  - Thur: STR
  - Fri: FIT

- Week 4: Mon: STR
  - Tue: FTS
  - Thur: FIT
  - Fri: FTS

If time's not on your side and you have ambitions in both the strength and fitness departments add a fusion session to strike at both goals:

- Mon: STR
  - Wed: FIT
  - Fri: FTS

- Tue: STR
  - Thu: FIT
  - Sat: FTS

When using a 'blocked' approach to your training organisation – focusing on certain elements for a given period – adding a FTS cycle will complete a very challenging program:

- Week 1–2: STR focus
  - Mon: STR
  - Wed: FIT
  - Fri: STR

- Week 3–4: FIT focus
  - Mon: FIT
  - Wed: STR
  - Fri: FIT

- Week 5–6: FTS focus
  - Mon: FTS
  - Wed: STR or FIT
  - Fri: FTS

If you haven't taken the advice set out earlier in this book and haven't put any plans in place, throw in a FTS session to break up the monotony of your regular routine.

PS:
Work on getting a plan in place. Training will be more efficient and results more forthcoming.

ONLY FOR THE BRAVE

Previous information on fusion training not enough to quench your thirst for aggressive training? Rather get out of the gym and do some work in the sun? I've got just the thing. Let's try adding EXTREME techniques to the mix.

Sled/tyre dragging circuit

A sled/tyre dragging session is a fantastic training mode to add to a FTS. A dragging session is massively challenging and can help increase:

- strength
- work capacity
- core stability.

Dragging sessions may be overloaded by simply adding a little extra weight, dragging for a little more distance or just picking up the speed a little. This makes for a massively demanding strength component to a fusion training session. Simply hook up a sled or tyre to a couple of pieces of rope.

Dragging is best combined with running when used in the context of a fusion training session.

Session 1

ORDER	EXERCISE	CONTENT	TIME
A	Running	2 x 800 m @ Zone 4 (approximately < 2:30 – 2:40) 1 min recovery	8 min
B	Dragging	1 x 50 m Chest Press – no Recovery 1 x 50 m Alternating Single Arm Row – 90 sec recovery	6 min
C	Running	3 x 400 m @ Zone 4 (approx. < 80 sec) 1 min recovery	7.5 min
D	Dragging	1 x 50 m Front Raise – no recovery 1 x 50 m Triceps Extension – 90 sec recovery	6 min
E	Running	2 x 800 m @ Zone 4 (approximately < 2:30 – 2:40) 1 min recovery	8 min
F	Dragging	1 x 50 m Lateral Raise (25 m each arm) – no recovery 1 x 50 m Woodchop (25 m each side)	6 min
TOTAL TIME			41.5 min

THESE TRAINING ELEMENTS ARE JUST THE TIP OF THE ICEBERG. GET CREATIVE AND ADD IN YOUR OWN COMPONENTS: FOR EXAMPLE, A MOUNTAIN BIKE OR PARACHUTE RUN.

HOW SIMPLE CAN IT BE?

A few years ago I had the odd knee problem which limited the amount of running I could do. My solution – drag my sled up the hill out the front of Mum and Dad's place using the exercises listed above. Then I'd hop on my sister's mountain bike and go for a 10 min sprint over the hills of the golf course that backed on to our street. As the course was privately owned I often had the added 'training stimulus' of security guards and dogs chasing me.

Partner sessions – competition (FTS Skins)

While some people go to the gym and get into their own little world, some like others to be around for motivation. Having like-minded souls about allows you to let loose the natural drive that's in all humans (especially males) – the need to WIN! FTS Skins is a fantastic session that will drive even the fittest to the brink of meltdown.

As with the sessions listed above FTS Skins is broken down into sets, with each set a Skin. While I'm no gambling man, putting a few bob on every Skin or betting the other person lunch adds plenty of spark to a session.

The winner of the each Skin is the person who performs best in the designated set, for example:

- **Skin 1:** 2 min rowing erg – greatest distance wins.

- **Skin 2:** 2 x 10 bench press – highest cumulative weight for both sets wins. If you fail to hit the reps prescribed you forfeit the set.

- **Skin 3:** 2 min boxing (focus pads) – person who achieves highest percentage of MHR wins. Skin is tied if both partners hit their MHR.

Tactics begins to play a role in the competition, as you have to weigh up factors like:

- If I go flat out to win this Skin will it burn me for the rest of the session?

- If I choose a weight that's too high I may not complete the prescribed reps and give the Skin away.

- Do I try to take him on in his 'pet' events and take a Skin off him forcing him to go hard on my good events, which he may be reluctant to do?

- Do I go hard early, try to get a few wins on the board and hopefully burn my mate by making him chase?

- Do I give him a few early and come home like a freight train?

**DECISIONS, DECISIONS …
NOW, FIND AN EQUALLY MAD MATE WHO'S LOOKING FOR VARIETY IN HIS TRAINING – AND WIN CASH OFF HIM!**

FLEXIBILITY
10 USE IT OR LOSE IT

Flexibility is the range of motion (ROM) of a given joint and is without question the most neglected part of fitness programs. It should be part of every regular fitness routine.

WHY IS FLEXIBILITY IMPORTANT?

Flexibility increases physical efficiency and performance. A flexible joint has the ability to move farther in its range and requires less energy to do so. Increasing this efficiency decreases the risk of injury, enabling various tissues and muscles to reach a maximum range during fitness activities. Flexibility also increases blood supply and nutrients to joint structures, which enhances the elasticity of tissues and muscles surrounding the joints of the body. Another plus is that increased flexibility allows freedom of movement

- Habitually using certain muscle groups within a small or restricted range of movement overactivates those particular muscle groups, which tends to shorten the muscle, thereby limiting the movement even further.
- Large muscle groups such as the gluteals and pectorals may be exercised in a limited range and become so tight that they cause postural problems or muscle imbalances. This is typically seen in 'meat-heads' who do too much bench pressing and end up with a caved-in chest.

which decelerates the degeneration of joints and will prolong your sporting life. Flexibility also delays muscular fatigue and prevents and alleviates muscle soreness after exercising.

USE IT OR LOSE IT

People neglect flexibility for one of two reasons:

1 Lack of knowledge. You didn't know it was important.

2 Lack of planning. You knew it was important but you brushed it off anyway.

Muscle adapts to changes in its length over a period of time. Stretching once or twice contributes to improvements, but ultimately it is *consistency* that achieves results.

Flexibility means different things to different people. For people whose body tends to be very tight, flexibility is a very important part of their program. However, for people who are very flexible naturally, an extensive flexibility program is not always the most appropriate activity to pursue as their bodies require greater stability. This is clearly explained in *Fix Your Back* (see 'Resources' on p 215).

Flexibility is truly a 'use it or lose it' commodity. An old martial arts master once told me: 'Every day you stretch you will get better, but miss one day and you will go backwards.' This isn't too far off the truth.

THE MECHANICS OF FLEXIBILITY OR RANGE OF MOVEMENT (ROM)

Structural limitations of the joint

Joints are made up of the ends of two bones, the cartilage between these and a capsule that surrounds the entire structure. Limitations within the joint itself that come from either an injury or genetic predisposition can limit range of movement around a joint. You should never attempt to stretch beyond the range of movement allowed by a joint. If you feel a 'bony' block toward the end of a movement you should restrict your flexibility to that point and have the joint assessed by a medical practitioner if you are unsure or it feels uncomfortable.

Mechanical properties of the muscles and soft tissues

Muscle shape and size varies both within and between individuals. Therefore a stretch that works for one person may not work for another simply because the second person's musculature is slightly differently orientated.

Excessive soft tissue in the form of body fat may prove a significant hurdle for some people when it comes to improving flexibility. At the other end of the scale, advanced levels of musculature may restrict some joints (for example, large biceps restrict the elbow joint).

In general, large musculature should not be blamed for restricted ROM. Muscles must be 'long and strong' in order to provide the performance they were designed for. Becoming big and bulky may serve to appease your fragile male ego, but ultimately you are looking at performance, and strength without ROM is untenable. Muscles that are forced into becoming shorter via high strength loads and neglected flexibility are considerably vulnerable to the risk of injury and limit flexibility.

Neuromuscular control of muscle length and tension

All muscular function (length and tension) is controlled by the central nervous system (CNS). The interaction between the CNS and the muscle is described (very simplistically) as the neuromuscular system. While the neuromuscular system provides the drive for contractile processes it also provides a protective mechanism that prevents – via muscular contraction – excessive or dangerous ROM being achieved around a particular joint.

An important psychological point to understand is that the body is a *homeostatic* beast. It doesn't like to be moved too far out of its comfort zone. Herein lies the key to training adaptation: moving the body a designated amount out of its comfort zone and allowing it sufficient time to recover forces it to adapt. Therefore, muscles that have been short and tight for a long time are going to need to be 'convinced' to change their length by both consistent application of the training stimulus and the use of a few tricks that will override the body's drive to remain in its comfort zone.

Proprioceptive Neuromuscular Facilitation (PNF) is the most effective way to trick the body into reducing the neural drive to a muscle thereby allowing it to attain an increased functional ROM. While the name of this technique and the reasons for its effectiveness are complex, the technique itself is quite simple. The example below is based on the hamstring group; however, the same principles can be applied to any muscle group.

1 Lie on your back, head and neck relaxed, and bring one leg up with the knee locked using a towel or belt to hold the position. At this point a gentle stretch should be felt. Hold for 30–60 sec.
2 Using the belt to hold your leg in place, contract your hamstring against it at approximately 60 per cent effort for 10–20 sec.
3 Relax (5 sec).
4 Actively contract your quad, attempting to pull the straight leg back toward you. Simultaneously apply gentle pressure to the belt, bringing the leg further back and increasing the intensity of the stretch. Hold for 30–60 sec.
5 Repeat 2–3 times on both legs.

By contracting the muscle group in opposition to the muscle targeted for flexibility you are actually turning off (or at least vastly reducing) the neural drive to the targeted muscle. Think about it for a minute – as one muscle contracts, the muscle on the opposite side must relax in order for movement to occur. Push–pull physics at its simplistic best!

Traditionally, PNF stretches are performed with a partner. Done using the method described above, they can be executed equally as effectively solo.

Based on the neural innervation (or stimulation) of a muscle, neglect may manifest itself in different ways. Without getting into the gory neurophysiological details, some muscles react to neglect (either insufficient or excessive use) by shortening and tightening (phasic neural innervation), while others react by lengthening and weakening (tonic neural innervation). Those muscles that shorten and tighten (most of the big ones) must be given appropriate stimulus to encourage them to retain their length. This is where flexibility/ROM training comes in.

A further consideration when addressing the function of large powerful muscle groups is the balance between increases in training volume or intensity and increases in flexibility training. Typically, as training loads increase, ROM training is discarded to make way for what is perceived as more important training means. However, the conundrum is that while increased training loads may contribute to more advanced work capacities, neglecting effective ROM training will greatly increase the risk of injury, as muscles shorten and tighten and cause the athlete to operate in an ever decreasing ROM.

THE PAIN, THE PAIN...

Flexibility training is not necessarily the most comfortable pastime in the world. That said, it should not be torture. Remember, the aim is to be consistent; if it is intolerably painful you will not do it regularly. Each person finds the point at which they are comfortable to stretch. As long as you continue to challenge the length of your muscles on a regular basis you will find your functional ROM improving.

Flexibility exercises

You should never do flexibility exercises without a proper warm up. When your body is cold the muscles and joints are at a greater risk of injury. A general warm up should consist of a 5-min period of low intensity aerobic activity (see p 47). You should aim to do your flexibility exercises before and after training.

For the most part I have given you an idea of the training modes and exercises that will most benefit from each stretch. However, there are a number of stretches that are ideal if you have been sitting for extended periods of time (for example, at work). Sitting for long periods contributes directly to many of the general back problems seen in otherwise healthy individuals.

In this day and age most people spend large portions of the day sitting in front of computers or driving, holding their bodies in positions for significant periods, contributing to unnecessary muscle soreness, poor joint function and therefore reduced athletic performance. Check out the 'Spark up' stretches on p 138 for a simple method to reduce the negative effects of long days at the office (or driving).

Following are 20 of the most effective stretches to help maintain your flexibility.

SIMPLE RULE: AN INCREASE IN OVERALL TRAINING REQUIRES AN INCREASE IN FLEXIBILITY/ROM TRAINING.

TRAIN TOUGH

1 DOG POSE (ADAPTED FROM YOGA)

This exercise stretches the nerves that run down the back of the leg and into the foot (sciatic and posterior tibial) and gives a nice hit on the calves.

- Position yourself with feet placed slightly wider than shoulder width, with your toes turned in slightly in your hands placed approximately 1–1.5 m in front of you.

- Lock your knees, then, using your hands push your hips back over your heels while dropping the shoulders. The sensation when done correctly should be quite strong and extend down the leg and into the foot (particularly if you are tight).

Associated with: Running/walking-related activities.

2 SLUMP

This exercise stretches the posterior neural chain from the cervical plexus (top) to the common peroneal and tibial nerves (bottom).

- Sit with your legs stretched out in front of you. Place one foot on top of the other. Make sure your feet are pointing up towards the ceiling. Place your hands behind your head, elbows out.

- Slump forward and collapse your chest.

- Use your hands to gently bring your head towards your knee.

- Release your head, and look toward your feet as you pull your toe back. Then pull the head down while pointing the toe away from you.

- Alternate this action in 5–15 sec cycles to get the best effect. The stretch may be felt anywhere down the chain depending on where you are tight.

Associated with: Running/walking-related activities, lower body strength loads.

3 LOWER LIMB NEURAL

This exercise specifically stretches the outside of the lower part of the knee and the lower leg.

■ Lie on your back with both legs out straight.

■ Hook a flexibility strap or belt around the arch of one foot and slowly bring your leg up to the vertical, as far as is comfortable.

■ Keeping your hips flat to the floor, move the upright leg across the midline of your body. This will be a relatively small movement. Keep pulling down on the side of the strap closest to your inner leg as you allow your foot to roll inwards. A sharp sensation should be felt to the outside of the knee. Point your foot; pull it up repeatedly against the strap for best effect.

Associated with: Running/walking-related activities, lower body strength loads.

4 STRAIGHT LEG CALF

This exercise stretches the upper calf.

■ Kneel with your hands shoulder-width apart.

■ Straighten your legs and place one foot on the floor with your heel flat on the floor.

■ Hook the other foot around the back of the ankle of the straight leg. Keep this leg slightly bent.

■ Keep your knee locked, and move the bent knee as far forward toward the floor as possible without unhooking your foot from around the ankle. The sensation of stretch may extend from mid-calf to the back of the knee.

Associated with: Running, stepping/stairs, lower body strength.

TRAINING TIPS

■ Nerves, like muscles have the capacity to shorten under excessive training load. Therefore they should be exercised and stretched regularly to ensure sound performance.

■ Neural stretches are not pleasant to do but achieve a good result. The sensation associated with them is generally intense. Breathe deeply through the discomfort and try to achieve as much range of motion as possible.

NB: Anyone with specific sciatic pain or known vertebral disc injuries should seek medical advice before completing any stretches of this nature.

5 BENT LEG CALF

This exercise stretches the lower calf.

■ Get yourself into the same position as for the Straight Leg Calf stretch.

■ Instead of locking the supporting leg, bend it slightly. This will change the stretch sensation to the lower part of your calf. You can put a small wedge under your toes to deepen the stretch.

Associated with: Running, stepping/stairs, lower body strength.

6 QUAD/HIP FLEXOR

This exercise stretches the quads (front of the thigh) across both knees and hips, and to a lesser extent, deep hip flexor musculature.

■ Get yourself into an upright kneeling position. Bend one knee up to a 90-degree angle and keep your foot flat on the floor.

■ Bend the other leg, lifting your foot up towards your buttocks. Keep your hips and shoulders straight, not twisted towards the lifted foot.

■ Push forward with your hips towards the front of the room, while keeping your tailbone pointing down, not lifting towards the back of the room. This will increase the stretch on the hip flexors. Some of you may find it easier to start this exercise by putting the back foot up onto a small box before attempting to bring their foot up.

Associated with: Sprinting, squatting/lunging, leg raises, extended sitting.

7 LONG PSOAS (PINCHED FROM MY GOOD FRIEND ANNA-LOUISE BOUVIER)

This exercise specifically stretches the deep hip flexors (psoas, or the muscle that lifts up the knee).

■ Get yourself into an upright kneeling position. Bend one knee up to a 90-degree angle and keep your foot flat on the floor.

■ Extend your back leg, resting on the balls of your toes. Keep your hips and shoulders square.

■ Lean over your bent leg in a lunge and place your hands on either side of your foot for balance.

■ Bend the outstretched leg slightly and squeeze your glutes 'through' the stretch. Try to keep your back as straight as you can without hunching over.

Associated with: Sprinting, squatting/lunging, leg raises, extended sitting.

8 GENERAL HIP FLEXOR

This exercise stretches the deep and superficial hip flexors (muscles that lift up the knee).

- Get yourself into an upright kneeling position. Bend one knee up to a 90-degree angle and keep your foot flat on the floor.

- Extend your back leg, resting on the balls of your toes. Keep your hips and shoulders square.

- Place both hands on the top of your bent knee and slowly push forward with your hips, opening the hips up. Squeeze your glutes 'through' the stretch. Try to keep your body upright and your tailbone down.

Associated with: Sprinting, squatting/lunging, leg raises, extended sitting.

TRAINING TIP

Sitting for a long period of time will shorten and tighten the muscles that lift your knees up. When you sit those muscles may be stimulated to contract. Consequently when you want to stand up, you may feel as though you are being pulled down at the front of your hips. Well, guess what? You are! This may further manifest itself as a stiff and sore lower back. Regular flexibility work on these muscles (stretches 6–8 above) reduces these ill effects of sitting.

9 GENERAL GLUTES

This exercise stretches the largest of the glute muscles, the gluteus maximus muscle.

- Sit yourself on the floor in a cross-legged position. Bend one leg in front of your body at a 45-degree angle. Extend the other leg out behind you, keeping your balance with your toe tip.

- Place your hands on either side of the bent leg for more stability.

- Keep your chest up and push forward with your sternum to enhance the stretch.

- For a more advanced version, bend forward, taking your chest to the floor over the bent leg.

Associated with: Sprinting, squatting/lunging, leg raises, extended sitting.

10 POSTERIOR CHAIN

This exercise simultaneously stretches the muscles running up the back of the upper thigh (hamstrings), across the hip (glutes) and into the back (spinal erectors).

- Lie on your back with both legs out straight.

- Hook a flexibility strap or belt around the arch of one foot and, holding the strap in one hand, slowly bring your leg up to the vertical, as far as is comfortable.

- Keep your leg straight as you take it across your body as close to the floor as possible.

- Make sure your upper back and shoulders stay flat on the floor. You can extend the opposite arm to the raised leg flat to the floor to anchor your body.

Associated with: Excellent general stretch for any activity involving the lower body.

11 STRAIGHT LEG HAMSTRING

This exercise stretches the rear of the upper thigh (hamstring musculature), and the top of the calf.

- Lie on your back with both legs out straight.

- Hook a flexibility strap or belt around the arch of one foot and, holding the strap in both hands, slowly bring your leg up to the vertical, as far as is comfortable.

- Keeping the knee locked, gently pull the leg back towards your body.

Associated with: Sprinting, running, squatting/lunging.

12 BENT KNEE HAMSTRING

This exercise stretches the rear of the upper thigh (the hamstring musculature).

- Lie on your back with both legs out straight.

- Hook a flexibility strap or belt around the arch of one foot and, holding the strap in both hands, slowly bring your leg up to the vertical, as far as is comfortable.

■ Bend the knee slightly as you gently pull the leg back towards your body. This stretch will be felt more in the middle/top of the hamstring.

Associated with: Sprinting, running, squatting/lunging.

13 ADDUCTOR

This exercise stretches the inner section of the upper thigh (the adductor musculature).

■ Lie on your back with both legs out straight.

■ Hook a flexibility strap or belt around the arch of one foot and, holding the strap in both hands, slowly bring your leg up to the vertical, as far as is comfortable.

■ Keeping the knee locked allow the leg to drop away from the body. Make sure that both hips stay flat to the floor.

Associated with: Change of direction running/agility, squatting/lunging.

14 THORACIC VERTEBRAE I

This exercise stretches the muscles that support and provide rotation to the mid to upper back (the thoracic vertebrae).

■ Sit with your legs stretched out in front of you.

■ Bend one leg and cross it over the straight leg.

■ Place the opposite arm to the bent leg on the outside of this leg. Keep your arm straight and the palm of this hand flat with the thumb pointing up.

■ Keep the chest held high and use your arm to lever the body around for the twist. Work towards having your upper body completely turned away from the straight leg.

Associated with: Heavy upper body lifting, deadlifting, extended sitting.

15 THORACIC VERTEBRAE II

This exercise stretches the muscles that support and provide rotation to the mid to upper back (the thoracic vertebrae).

- Get yourself into an upright kneeling position. Bend one knee up to a 90-degree angle and keep your foot flat on the floor.

- Place the opposite arm to the bent knee on the outside of this leg. Keep your arm straight and the palm of this hand flat.

- Use your arm to lever your body around for the twist. Raise the other arm up as high as you can get it. Work towards having your upper body completely turned away from the bent leg.

Associated with: Heavy upper body lifting, deadlifting, extended sitting.

16 LATS

This exercise stretches the big upper back muscles that wrap under your arm and down to the spine. Also know as the lats (latissimus dorsi).

- Kneel down on all fours and reach forward with your arms, keeping both hands flat on the floor.

- Move your feet slightly to the left and do the same with your hands. This will make your right side curve slightly sideways.

- Keep your hands anchored firmly to the floor and drag back slightly on your hands, pushing your buttocks towards the back wall. The stretch will be felt in the upper right hand side of the back (near the rear of the arm pit). Reverse to stretch the left side.

Associated with: Heavy upper body lifting (particularly with a back focus) and rowing.

TRAINING TIP

A typical overuse symptom of rowing (boat, scull or ergometer) is a tight lower back. Assuming there are no structural reasons for the pain, one of the simplest solutions is to stretch the lats hard. The latissimus dorsi muscle is the prime upper body muscle used in rowing, and is connected along a piece of connective tissue (thoraco-lumbar fascia) which wraps around the lower back. As the lats become tight from excessive use this is often felt in the lower back. Rowers beware!

17 GENERAL BACK

This exercise stretches the muscles of the upper back.

■ Kneel down on all fours.

■ Stretch one arm forward and bring the other arm across and under the outstretched arm, with the aim of getting your shoulder and head to the ground.

Associated with: nothing in particular … just feels good!

18 SHOULDER

This exercise stretches the muscles to the rear of the shoulder.

■ Stand straight and bring one arm up to shoulder height, stretching out to the front.

■ Bring the straight arm across your body, making sure that you keep your shoulders square and not following your arm.

■ Hook your other arm underneath the straight arm and use it to enhance the stretch.

■ Do the same with the other arm.

Associated with: Heavy upper body lifting (particularly with a back focus) and swimming.

19 CHEST

This exercise stretches the chest muscle (the pectoralis major).

■ Stand next to a solid structure that is taller than you.

■ Place your arm on the structure above shoulder height.

■ Keeping your hips and shoulders square, step through with your inside foot leaving the hand on the structure. You will feel a stretch across the chest.

Associated with: Heavy upper body lifting (particularly with a chest focus) and swimming.

TRAINING TIP

A typical overuse symptom of swimming is rounded shoulders. This happens as the chest muscles become stronger, often shortening and tightening, subsequently pulling the shoulders forward. This may result in irregular function of the shoulders and lead to other injuries associated with shoulder balance irregularities. Regular stretching of the chest, particularly in the 24 hours after heavy sessions, helps prevent this.

TRAIN TOUGH

20 TRICEP

This exercise stretches the triceps (muscles at the rear of the upper arm).

- Stand upright and hold a flexibility strap in one hand. Raise this arm straight above your head.

- Bend the arm down behind your head and neck, so that the strap dangles down your back.

- Grab hold of the bottom of the strap with your other hand and pull on it to increase the stretch on the top arm.

Associated with: Heavy pressing activity in the gym and swimming.

Stretch Combinations

Different combinations of stretches suit different activities. Not every stretch works the same for every person. Find the ones that increase your functional range of movement and stick with them.

Warm Up

Use these stretches in short bursts of 10–20 sec in association with light movement (enough to raise a sweat).

Cool Down

Given that training has caused muscle damage don't go too nuts. Hold stretches for approximately 20–40 sec, 2–3 times on your favourites.

Stretch Session

Aiming to improve the range of movement (flexibility) takes work like anything else. Use longer blocks of 60–90 sec, slowly increasing the tension on the muscles to improve range. Depending on what type of exercise you have done, use the following exercises as part of your stretch sessions. The numbers refer to the flexibility exercises listed above.

Running: 1–5, 7, 9, 10, 12
Sprinting: 1–13
Swimming: 2, 4, 7, 14, 16, 18–20
Rowing: 1, 2, 6, 7, 9, 10, 12, 15–18
Upper body strength: 15–20
Lower body strength: 2–14
Martial arts: 1–3, 6–14

TRAINING TIP
SPARK-UP STRETCHES: 1, 2, 7, 9, 14, 17, 19

Sleeping causes the body to tighten up quite a bit. Waking tight contributes to a feeling of fatigue and apathy in the morning. Hop in a warm shower for 5 min and then complete each of these stretches twice for 30 sec to get you out of the blocks.

Similarly, if you are feeling the mid-afternoon blues at work, give these a crack to get you sparked up.

PART 3
GOING FOR IT

GETTING OUT
OF THE BLOCKS

The aim of these programs is to increase the physical performance of the beginner across the board from basic level. They will increase general fitness and strength, providing a solid foundation in both. You will have to commit to three to six days a week to see results.

PERFORMANCE GOALS

Establishing your first series of goals is the hardest part about starting. As mentioned in Chapter 3, if you don't know where you are going, choosing the right road is hard, but not impossible. As you get used to your training program, your goals will probably change quite rapidly (depending on individual adaptation). Change your performance goals to suit where you are up to in your training, but always remember to keep them realistic. The basic aims of the Getting Out of the Blocks program are to increase:

- general strength

- aerobic fitness

- flexibility.

Make sure your doctor gives you a clean bill of health before engaging in any physical training program. It is crucial that you do not place yourself in any unnecessary risk by asking your body to do something that it's not up to.

Remember, the key to making a start is to set realistic goals. Keep them simple and achievable.

TESTS BEFORE YOU GET STARTED

Fat

- If you feel you need to lose fat, the most accurate way to know for sure is to have your fat levels assessed by a health professional. Most big universities run programs that allow people to have measurements taken for a small fee.

- Be aware of inaccurate assessment techniques in which plastic callipers are used, or little time is taken assessing the sample site.

- If you don't want to subject yourself to this test or can't find an appropriate professional, place a very clear mark on the inside of a belt you wear regularly. Use this mark to show any changes in your waist measurement. Better still, use a tape measure at the level of your belly button. This measurement corresponds quite well to reductions in body fat and will give you an easy assessment of your progress.

Weight

- Body weight should be measured at the start of a program like this, but don't rely solely on it as a measure of success.

- One of the primary aims of a body fat reduction program is to increase the level of *active* muscle tissue in the body. Muscles use energy whereas fat does not, thereby contributing to total energy expenditure for the day.

- The simple rule of thumb is: greater energy expenditure than energy consumption (eating) equals body fat loss.

- However, you need to stimulate muscle *growth* or weight loss will inevitably be in the form of muscle atrophy (wastage).

A MATTER OF FAT!

Have you ever known somebody who says they've lost 'X' number of kilos yet they still look fat? Well, that's what happens when you restrict your energy intake and go putting in marathon efforts running, walking or whatever. The commitment is admirable, but the methodology is a bit off-track. A strength-training program to stimulate muscle activation – thereby reducing the body's natural instinct to breakdown protein (muscle) in the face of a reduced energy diet – must be a part of a fat reduction program.

A real world fitness test

- Knowing your maximal volume of oxygen consumption (MVO_2), a score generated in most science-based fitness tests, is of little interest, so implement a simple real world test. For example, measure the time it takes you to:

  - jog or walk 5 km (easily done on a treadmill)

  - ride 8 to10 km (again, a stationary bike would make an accurate reading easier)

  - swim 1000 m.

Remember:
- These tests aren't a measure of what's good or bad – all you need to know is *what you can do*.

- The information generated from the above tests is a measure of your current performance and should be repeated in 6 weeks to measure your improvement.

- Initially these tests should be done at a pace that allows you to complete the selected test without undue stress. Don't push yourself too hard too soon.

TRAIN TOUGH

THE PROGRAMS

The First Steps (Weeks 1–4)

DAY		DAY	
Monday	Fitness	Friday	Fusion
Tuesday		Saturday	Fitness (optional)
Wednesday	Strength	Sunday	
Thursday			

NB: Repeat the fitness session if you want to tack an extra session on to the week. Similarly, an extra strength session may be added, provided there's a minimum of one day between strength sessions.

MONDAY

		WORK	INTENSITY	RECOVERY
WEEK 1	Set 1	4 x 10 min efforts XTR or Locomotion	Zone 1 (60–75% MHR)	90 sec
WEEK 2	Set 1	4 x 12 min efforts XTR or Locomotion	Zone 1	90 sec
WEEK 3	Set 1	3 x 15 min efforts XTR or Locomotion	Zone 1	90 sec
WEEK 4	Set 1	3 x 15 min efforts XTR or Locomotion	Zone 1	90 sec

NB:
- XTR equals cross training (for example, gym-based equipment); Locomotion equals outdoor activity (for example, running, walking, bike).
- When using XTR equipment change equipment on every effort to amplify challenge.
- See Chapter 5, 'Fitness' to work out your Zone 1 and MHR.

WEDNESDAY – Complete 1 to 2 times a week (depending on available time)

ORDER	EXERCISE	TEMPO	REC	WEEK 1	WEEK 2	WEEK 3	WEEK 4
A1	Body Weight Squats	3/1/1	N/A	3 x 10	3 x 12	4 x 12	2 x 12
A2	Push Ups	2/1/1	60 sec	3 x 10	3 x 12	4 x 12	2 x 12
B1	Turkish Get Ups	Controlled	N/A	3 x 4 each side	3 x 6 each side	4 x 6 each side	2 x 6 each side
B2	Pull Ups	2/1/1	60 sec	3 x 6	3 x 8	4 x 8	2 x 8
C1	Step Ups	3/1/1	N/A	3 x 10 each side	3 x 12 each side	4 x 12 each side	2 x 12 each side
C2	Plate Front Raise (5 kg)	2/2/2	60 sec	3 x 8	3 x 10	4 x 12	2 x 10

NB:
- Letters refer to the order in which exercises are completed – A, B, C, etc.
- Two exercises listed under the same letter are done together (Super Set) for example: A1 and A2 are completed together for detailed sets and reps; when completed move onto B1 and B2 (not the Bananas, sorry that's from having small children at home!).
- Tempo refers to the speed of execution of each exercise:
  - first number is the speed in seconds the lowering of the load
  - second number is the time in seconds the bottom position of the movement is held
  - third number is the speed in seconds the raising of the load.

FRIDAY

ORDER	EXERCISE	CONTENT	TIME
A	Bike/Treadmill/Orbit walker	2 x 3 min @ Zone 3 with 1 min recovery	8 min
B1	Push Ups	2 x 10 with 30 sec recovery	5 min
B2	UG Chin-ups	2 x 8 with 30 sec recovery	
C	Bike/Treadmill/Orbit walker	2 x 3 min @ Zone 3 with 1 min recovery	8 min
D1	Split Squat (no weight)	2 x 12 on each leg	5 min
D2	Burpees	2 x 10	
E	Bike/Treadmill/Orbit walker	2 x 3 min @ Zone 3 with 1 min recovery	8 min
F	CORE Circuit	Back Extensions 2 x 10 Cable Woodchop 2 x 10 each side Old School Sit Up 2 x 10	5 min
TOTAL TIME			**39 min**

TRAIN TOUGH

Up & Running (Weeks 5–8)

DAY		DAY	
Monday	Fitness	Friday	Fusion
Tuesday		Saturday	Fitness
Wednesday	Strength	Sunday	
Thursday			

MONDAY

		WORK	INTENSITY	RECOVERY
WEEK 5	Set 1	5 x 5 min efforts	Zone 2 (75%–85% MHR)	90 sec
WEEK 6	Set 1	7 x 4 min efforts	Zone 2	90 sec
WEEK 7	Set 1	2 x 5 min efforts	Zone 2	90 sec
	Set 2	5 x 2 min efforts	Zone 3 (85%–90% MHR)	60 sec
	Set 3	2 x 5 min efforts	Zone 2	90 sec
WEEK 8	Set 1	2 x 5 min efforts	Zone 2	90 sec
	Set 2	5 x 2 min efforts	Zone 3	60 sec
	Set 3	2 x 5 min efforts	Zone 3	90 sec

■ See Chapter 5, 'Fitness' to work out your Zone 2 and MHR

WEDNESDAY – Complete 1 to 2 times a week (depending on available time)

ORDER	EXERCISE	TEMPO	REC	WEEK 1	WEEK 2	WEEK 3	WEEK 4
A1	Single Leg Squat	3/1/1	N/A	3 x 6	3 x 8	4 x 8	2 x 8
A2	Push Ups	2/1/1	60 sec	3 x 12	3 x 15	4 x 15	2 x 15
B1	DB Turkish Get Ups	Controlled	N/A	3 x 6 each side	3 x 8 each side	4 x 8 each side	2 x 8 each side
B2	Pull Ups	2/1/1	60 sec	3 x 8	3 x 10	4 x 10	2 x 10
C1	Walking Lunge	3/1/1	N/A	3 x 8 each side	3 x 10 each side	4 x 10 each side	2 x 10 each side
C2	Plate Front Raise (10 kg)	2/2/2	60 sec	3 x 8	3 x 10	4 x 12	2 x 10

FRIDAY

ORDER	EXERCISE	CONTENT	TIME
A	Rowing Erg	2 x 2 min >550 m, recovery 1 min between sets	6 min
B	Strength Set	Squat 1 x 12 – no recovery Military Press 1 x 12 – 90 sec recovery	3.5 min
C	Rowing Erg	2 x 2 min >570m, recovery 1 min between sets	6 min
D	Strength Set	Deadlift 1 x 12 – no recovery Bench Press 1 x 12 – 90 sec recovery	3.5 min
E	Rowing Erg	2 x 2 min >590 m, 1 minute between sets	6 min
F	Strength Set	Split Squat 1 x 12 – no recovery Diesel Press 1 x 12 – 90 sec recovery	3.5 min
TOTAL TIME			**37.5 min**

NB:
- Letters refer to the order in which exercises are completed – A, B, C, etc.
- Two exercises listed under the same letter are done together (Super Set) for example: A1 and A2 are completed together for detailed sets and reps; when completed move onto B1 and B2.
- Tempo refers to the speed of execution of each exercise:
  - first number is the time in seconds to lower the weight
  - second number is the pause in seconds at the bottom of the movement
  - third number is the time in seconds to lift the weight

SATURDAY

		WORK	INTENSITY	RECOVERY
WEEK 5	Set 1	6 x 4 min efforts	Zone 2 (75%–85% MHR)	90 sec
WEEK 6	Set 1	10 x 3 min	Zone 2	60 sec
WEEK 7	Set 1	2 x 5 min	Zone 2	60 sec
		3 x 2 min Repeat x 2	Zone 3 (85%–95% MHR)	90 sec
WEEK 8	Set 1 Set 2 Set 3	2 x 5 min 3 x 3 min Repeat x 2	Zone 2 Zone 3	60 sec 90 sec

TRAIN TOUGH

NOT ENOUGH STRENGTH WORK ...

Listed below are 2 x two-day strength programs that may be completed during the Up and Running program (weeks 5–8). While the strength exercises in the first two programs listed above are unconventional, they will certainly provide a great base for moving onto more conventional programs like the ones below and those detailed in 'Muscle Up' on p 164. Give 'em a go.

Additional Strength Program 1
Day 1

ORDER	EXERCISE	TEMPO	REC	WEEK 1	WEEK 2	WEEK 3	WEEK 4
A	Front Squat	3/2/1	90 sec	3 x 12	3 x 10	3 x 8	2 x 8
B	Back Extension	2/2/2	90 sec	3 x 12	3 x 10	3 x 8	2 x 8
C	Single Leg Bridge	2/2/2	90 sec	3 x 12	3 x 10	3 x 8	2 x 8
D	Pulldowns OH F	3/2/1	90 sec	3 x 12	3 x 10	3 x 8	2 x 8
E	DB Shoulder Press	3/2/1	90 sec	3 x 12	3 x 10	3 x 8	2 x 8
F	Bench Press	3/2/1	90 sec	3 x 12	3 x 10	3 x 8	2 x 8
G	Dips	3/2/1	90 sec	3 x 12	3 x 10	3 x 8	2 x 8
H	EZY Bar Curl	3/2/1	90 sec	3 x 12	3 x 10	3 x 8	2 x 8

Day 2

ORDER	EXERCISE	TEMPO	REC	WEEK 1	WEEK 2	WEEK 3	WEEK 4
A	Squat	3/2/1	90 sec	3 x 12	3 x 10	3 x 8	2 x 8
B	DB Romanian Deadlift	2/2/2	90 sec	3 x 12	3 x 10	3 x 8	2 x 8
C	Supine TB Curl	2/2/2	90 sec	3 x 10	3 x 12	3 x 15	2 x 15
D	Bent Over Row UH	3/2/1	90 sec	3 x 12	3 x 10	3 x 8	2 x 8
E	Incline DB Press	3/2/1	90 sec	3 x 12	3 x 10	3 x 8	2 x 8
F	Behind Neck Press	3/2/1	90 sec	3 x 12	3 x 10	3 x 8	2 x 8
G	CG Push Ups	3/2/1	90 sec	3 x 12	3 x 10	3 x 8	2 x 8
H	DB Hammer Curl	3/2/1	90 sec	3 x 12	3 x 10	3 x 8	2 x 8

Additional Strength Program 2
Day 1

ORDER	EXERCISE	TEMPO	REC	WEEK 1	WEEK 2	WEEK 3	WEEK 4
A	Front Squat	3/2/1	90 sec	3 x 12	3 x 10	3 x 8	2 x 8
B	Deadlift	2/2/2	90 sec	3 x 12	3 x 10	3 x 8	2 x 8
C	Single Leg Bridge	2/2/2	90 sec	3 x 12	3 x 10	3 x 8	2 x 8
D1	Chin-ups OH F	3/2/1	N/A	3 x 12	3 x 10	3 x 8	2 x 8
D2	DB Shoulder Press	3/2/1	90 sec	3 x 12	3 x 10	3 x 8	2 x 8
E	Bench Press	3/2/1	90 sec	3 x 12	3 x 10	3 x 8	2 x 8
F1	Dips	3/2/1	N/A	3 x 12	3 x 10	3 x 8	2 x 8
F2	CG Bench Press	3/2/1	90 sec	3 x 12	3 x 10	3 x 8	2 x 8

Day 2

ORDER	EXERCISE	TEMPO	REC	WEEK 1	WEEK 2	WEEK 3	WEEK 4
A	Squat	3/2/1	90 sec	3 x 12	3 x 10	3 x 8	2 x 8
B	Romanian Deadlift	2/2/2	90 sec	3 x 12	3 x 10	3 x 8	2 x 8
C	Supine TB Curl	2/2/2	90 sec	3 x 10	3 x 12	3 x 15	2 x 15
D1	Bent Over Row UH	3/2/1	N/A	3 x 12	3 x 10	3 x 8	2 x 8
D2	Incline DB Press	3/2/1	90 sec	3 x 12	3 x 10	3 x 8	2 x 8
E	Single Arm Row	3/2/1	90 sec	3 x 12	3 x 10	3 x 8	2 x 8
F1	EZY Bar Curl	3/2/1	N/A	3 x 12	3 x 10	3 x 8	2 x 8
F2	DB Hammer Curl	3/2/1	90 sec	3 x 12	3 x 10	3 x 8	2 x 8

12 FIT 'N' FAST

One of the best reasons for being in good physical shape is to be competitive on the field of battle, to stand alongside your team-mates and crash headlong into the fiery path of the opposition.

While not every team sport evokes mental pictures of *Braveheart*-type battles, there's no doubt that once the whistle blows most people are keen to do what it takes to win the game. Team sports come in many different shapes and sizes, but the factors that contribute to physical success in any given field sport have common elements.

REPEATED EXPLOSIVE SPEED

Success at team field sport is generally based on the ability to apply accurate and appropriate skills at the highest speed possible. However, unlike a sprinter, a field sport player has to be capable of maintaining the highest possible percentage of his maximum acceleration and velocity for efforts that may vary from 5 m to greater than 50 m for the duration of a game, all with varied periods of recovery.

COMBATIVE STRENGTH

Static engagements (scrums, lineouts) and more dynamic engagements (tackling, cleanouts, hit-ups, the rucking duel) are all based on the rapid application of the greatest possible force in an unpredictable and fluid environment. While this is primarily the domain of full-contact football codes, sports such as soccer and hockey have numerous combative strength elements, particularly when competing for the ball.

RUNNING EFFICIENCY

While all field sport is won and lost based on what a team can do *with* the ball, ultimately the team that wins generally works the hardest off the field. How many times have you heard coaches talking about the 'one-percenters' of getting into position, running decoy lines, providing support in attack and defence, shepherding, and so on? Players who move *efficiently* at speeds less than their maximum fatigue themselves less, thereby sustaining the energy necessary to apply repeated explosive speed at critical parts of the game.

Every pre-season, somebody, somewhere, will spout the newest and greatest method for getting players ready. The interesting thing about this type of talk is that, technology aside, there really aren't any new training techniques. For the most part those who claim to possess the newest and greatest techniques are dredging up old sessions and invigorating them with words like 'specificity'. (I know this because I'm one of 'em!)

WHAT IS SPECIFICITY?

In a nutshell, it means that you need to *train in a manner as close to that in which you compete* in order to have the greatest effect on your competitive performance.

150

TRAIN FAST, BE FAST

The vast majority of a field sport player's training needs to be conducted above 80 per cent maximum speed. Ultimately, you're a product of what you do. If you spend years doing long runs on your own you'll inevitably be a slow player. You may be able to go all day but you'll be largely ineffective when it comes to applying repeated speed efforts such as making breaks, try-saving tackles, six-bounces-and-a-goal-from-outside-fifty, and so on.

That said, it's critical that field sport players have plenty of running in their legs. In order to tolerate the time required to complete team and individual training sessions, you must be capable of sustaining a solid volume of work. During a game of rugby, for instance, players might cover between 5 to 8 km depending on their position. Some AFL players will run twice that. Training sessions may involve similar volumes. You've got to be able to do this, at speed, every time, at practice or play.

NB: Being truly competitive on the field involves being physiologically fit (strong oxygen delivery and lactate removal system) as well as being bio-mechanically strong (strong and enduring stability musculature around the pelvis, durable muscles and tendons of the lower limbs).

Here's a quick rundown of the most common methods of field sports training.

Long slow distance running

This is generally used as a method of recovery and regeneration. It is excellent for:

- developing base running/strength/endurance in stability muscles around the hip and lower leg

- long-term changes to structural elements of the oxygen delivery system (you'll have more wind)

- developing a higher lactate threshold and running efficiency in athletes required to compete over longer distances, for example, AFL. The slight disadvantage is that running velocities contribute little to speed.

A WORD FROM THE COACH

While I certainly enjoy going for a run myself, I tend not to use this technique for distances greater than 3 to 4 km for most players. It's great during the summer months for footballers to get out and run in social environments, like the beach, and sustain their running fitness while checking out the new season bikinis on show!

TRAIN TOUGH

Intervals

Taking differing duration breaks between a variety of efforts conducted at higher speeds (for example, 4 x 4 min efforts @ 85 per cent, 90 sec rest between efforts) was popularised by Finnish runners in the early 1950s. This technique is fantastic for developing the mechanics and physiology of running.

NB: Running efficiently over a sustained period (particularly where repeated efforts are required) requires the athlete's physiology and running mechanics to be in order for optimal performance to be produced. Interval training promotes increased energy production via both aerobic and anaerobic means when compared to a single-paced long run, that is, improved physiology. Similarly, because the pace of interval running is greater than that of single-paced long running, running muscles are conditioned to handle greater levels of speed production via increased intra- and inter-musculature coordination. Therefore, the average running pace of the athlete is raised as a function of greater mechanical efficiency.

Interval sessions are designed according to several related variables:

- **Length:** Longer intervals tend to stress maximal oxygen consumption, while shorter ones stress the production and removal of lactic acid.

- **Speed:** The speed of the interval will determine how repeatable an effort is. High-speed intervals tend to require greater recovery, while lower speed intervals can be of a longer duration with lower recovery.

- **Density:** Longer recovery obviously allows more time for a blow, but therefore fewer intervals per session (**Density is lowered**). Shorter recovery periods allow less recovery and *amplify* the effect of the length of the rep by completing more reps per session (**Density is raised**). The number of reps in succession amplifies the effect. Fewer reps completed in succession allows greater emphasis on speed, while a greater number allows more emphasis to be placed on the physiological stress of the interval. In simple terms the greater the density of a session the greater the amount of work done in a given period of time.

Session 1 (Low Density)
10 x 2 min efforts @ 75 per cent MHR / 2 min recovery = 40 min total

Session 2 (High Density)
10 x 2 min efforts @ 75 per cent MHR / 1 min recovery = 30 min total
(Volume and Intensity are the same as Session 1, but reducing recovery between sets has increased the rate of work done and therefore increased session density)

Session 3 (High Density)
5 x 4 min efforts @ 75 per cent MHR / 2 min recovery = 30 min total
(Volume, intensity and recovery are the same as Session 1, but increasing the interval length has increased the rate of work done and therefore increased session density.)

■ **Volume:** The faster the interval speed the shorter the overall session, while the slower the speed the greater the potential for volume overload. Total volume of the session also contributes to the overall tolerance of the individual to distances encountered in the competitive environment. Specific sport and positional requirements dictate the total volume of the session required.

Single Session Volume Maximums

(General sport estimates only – specifics must be established depending on your individual training history … . If you're only just starting out, don't go out and try to knock these over.)

AFL:	3 km – 10 km
Soccer:	2 km – 8 km
Rugby:	2 km – 5 km
Basketball:	1.5 km – 4 km

Interval training is broadly classified into two types.

1 Extensive intervals

These tend to be longer in nature (approximately 300 m to 1000 m), emphasising development of maximal oxygen consumption, lactate clearance, sustained running efficiency and lactic acid tolerance. Recovery periods in these types of intervals tend to be inversely proportional, meaning as the interval gets longer, the recovery gets shorter.

For example:

■ Longer intervals / less recovery:
4 x 1000 m
- complete in < 4:30 min
- recovery 90 sec

■ Shorter intervals / more recovery:
2 x (4 x 400 m)
- complete in < 75 sec
- recovery 2 min between reps
- recovery 4 min between sets

2 Intensive intervals

These focus primarily on the development of repeated speed ability, and lactic acid production and tolerance, utilising shorter distances (10 m to 300 m). Longer periods of recovery allow for greater emphasis on speed. Shorter recovery places more stress on lactic acid tolerance, oxygen uptake and so on.

For example:

■ Lower density / greater speed focus / more recovery
- 2 x (4 x 100 m)
- complete each rep in < 15 sec
- recovery between reps 90 sec
- recovery between sets 3 min

■ Higher density / greater metabolic stress / less recovery
- 2 x (10 x 50 m)
- complete each rep in < 7.5 sec
- start reps every 25 sec
- recovery between sets 2 min

Speed

To the ambitious field sport athlete this is the Holy Grail! Speed is the most devastating weapon in any field sport. Some coaches will tell you it's impossible to make speed gains. Two words: bull shit! While I agree true gas is born not made, every athlete can improve his or her speed by addressing it on a regular basis.

Speed should be worked into your program based on a three-part model:

1 **Tempo Running:** Longer efforts (up to 100 m) completed at approximately 80 per cent effort. Try to develop rhythm and efficiency in your running dynamics, condition your musculature to tolerate higher velocities and reinforce 'relaxed' application of effort. Tempo running can also be used in the later stages of warm up.

2 **Maximum Efforts:** Typically shorter efforts (up to 50 m) aimed at developing acceleration and maximum speed. Should be executed when as physically fresh as possible in order to achieve the best results. Recovery periods should be maximised, allowing the neuromuscular system to prepare optimally for the next rep. Think of the neuromuscular system as a set of spark plugs with limited charge. They can only be asked to go flat out for a short period of time before they require a rest. When attempting to improve the ability to achieve maximal running speed, recovery periods of between 2–5 min may be required to allow the spark plugs to charge up again.

3 **Agility:** This involves the sport-specific application of speed. Drills must be implemented based on the requirements of the sport. Sit down and have a think about the patterns you sprint in your game and then simply use them in your training drills. Do you need to sidestep? Swerve? Somersault?

Speed technique is a complicated proposition to coach on the field, let alone from a book. Listed below are some standard points to think about during your running sessions. If you're serious about improving your technique take the time to join your local athletic club and get some specific coaching.

Maximum speed:
- Always run relaxed. A relaxed muscle moves faster than a tense one.
- Your arms should be flexed at roughly 90 degrees at the elbow with the hands lightly flexed.
- Drive your arms from the shoulders, with the hands coming to the level of the face in front and behind the plane of your gluteal muscles at the rear (running 'cheek-to-cheek').
- Your knee should drive through, with the foot at about the height of the opposite knee, toes held up.
- Lean your body slightly forward.

Acceleration:
- Focus on aggressive arm drive (particularly backwards).
- Drive forward and hard with your knees.
- Your back leg must finish fully extended.
- Shoulders should be well forward of the hips. Picture an imaginary straight line extending from ankle to ear.

If you feel that you are really behind the eight ball in terms of your fitness, picking up extra sessions in the gym on cross training equipment (rowing erg, orbit walker, etc) will help add additional load to your training. This will also reduce the draining effect of higher volume runs on your legs, allowing you to be fresher for the more specific task of running fast.

MOST FIELD SPORTS ARE RUNNING GAMES

To play well you must be able to run well. On the strength front the same applies: intensity is key! Maintaining a training level that is at a high percentage of your maximum allows for greater development of the fast twitch fibres which translates to speed and power.

THE PROGRAMS

DAY		DAY	
Monday	Strength	Friday	Strength
Tuesday		Saturday	Fitness
Wednesday	Fitness	Sunday	
Thursday			

MONDAY

ORDER	EXERCISE	TEMPO	REC	WEEK 1	WEEK 2	WEEK 3	WEEK 4	WEEK 5	WEEK 6
A	Front Squat	3/1/1	90 sec	2 x 12	2 x 8	2 x 10	2 x 6	2 x 8	2 x 6
B	Deadlift	2/2/2	90 sec	4 x 8	4 x 6	2 x 8	4 x 4	4 x 6	2 x 4
C	Good Morning	2/2/2	90 sec	3 x 8	3 x 6	2 x 8	3 x 4	3 x 6	2 x 4
D1	Chin-ups OH F (add weight as reps get lower)	3/0/1	N/A	3 x 12	4 x 8	3 x 10	4 x 6	4 x 8	3 x 6
D2	Military Press	3/1/1	90 sec	3 x 12	4 x 8	2 x 10	4 x 6	4 x 8	2 x 6
E	Bench Press	3/1/1	90 sec	3 x 12	3 x 8	2 x 10	3 x 6	3 x 8	2 x 6
F1	EZY Bar Curl	3/1/1	N/A	2 x 12	2 x 8	2 x 10	2 x 6	2 x 8	2 x 6
F2	DB Hammer Curl	3/1/1	90 sec	2 x 12	2 x 8	2 x 10	2 x 6	2 x 8	2 x 6

Lift tempo: This defines the speed at which the lift is completed. The first number is the time in seconds to lower the weight, the second is the pause in seconds at the bottom of the movement, and the third number is the time in seconds to lift the weight.

TRAIN TOUGH

WEDNESDAY

		WORK	INTENSITY	RECOVERY
WEEK 1	Set 1	3 x (10 x 100 m on 60 sec)	Finish in 14–16 sec	3 min between sets
WEEK 2	Set 1 Set 2	5 x 200m on 30 sec 2 x (10 x 100 m on 60 sec)	Finish in 32–36 sec Finish in 14–16 sec	3 min between sets
WEEK 3	Set 1 Set 2	10 x 200 m on 2 min 10 x 100 m on 60 sec	Finish in 32–36 sec Finish in 14–16 sec	3 min between sets
WEEK 4	Set 1	4 x 60 m – Tempo runs	80% effort – focus on rhythm!	Walk back between each rep. 3 min rest before Set 2
	Set 2	10 x 20 m – Speed	100%	2 min between each rep
WEEK 5	Set 1	3 x 60 m – Tempo runs	80% effort – focus on rhythm!	Walk back between each rep. 3 min rest before Set 2
	Set 2	6 x 20 m – Speed	100%	2 min between each rep
	Set 3	8 x 10 m – Speed	100%	2 min between each rep
WEEK 6	Set 1	4 x 50 m –Tempo runs	80% effort – focus on rhythm!	Walk back between each rep. 3 min rest before Set 2
	Set 2	5 x 20 m – Speed	100%	2 min between each rep
	Set 3	5 x 10m – Speed	100 %	2 min between each rep

FRIDAY

ORDER	EXERCISE	TEMPO	REC	WEEK 1	WEEK 2	WEEK 3	WEEK 4	WEEK 5	WEEK 6
A	Squat or Split Squat	3/2/1	90 sec	3 x 10	3 x 8	2 x 10	3 x 6	2 x 8	2 x 6
B	Romanian Deadlift	2/2/2	90 sec	3 x 8	3 x 6	2 x 8	3 x 6	3 x 4	2 x 4
C1	Bent Over Row UH	3/2/1	N/A	3 x 12	3 x 8	3 x 10	3 x 6	3 x 8	2 x 6
C2	Incline DB Press	3/2/1	90 sec	3 x 12	3 x 8	2 x 10	3 x 6	3 x 8	2 x 6
D	DB Shrug	3/2/1	90 sec	3 x 12	3 x 8	2 x 10	3 x 6	4 x 8	2 x 6
E1	Dips	3/2/1	N/A	3 x 12	3 x 8	2 x 10	3 x 6	3 x 8	2 x 6
E2	CG Bench Press	3/2/1	90 sec	3 x 12	3 x 8	2 x 10	3 x 6	2 x 8	2 x 6
F2	DB Hammer Curl	3/1/1	90 sec	2 x 12	2 x 8	2 x 10	2 x 6	2 x 8	2 x 6

SATURDAY

		WORK	INTENSITY	RECOVERY
WEEK 1	Set 1	6 x 4 min (try to maintain distance on each effort)	Zone 3 (85–90 % MHR)	1 min between sets
WEEK 2	Set 1	5 x 5 min (try to maintain distance on each effort)	Zone 3	1 min between sets
WEEK 3	Set 1	4 x 7 min (try to maintain distance on each effort)	Zone 3	1 min between sets
WEEK 4	Set 1	3 x (10 x 100 m on 60 sec)	Finish in 14–16 sec	3 min between sets
WEEK 5	Set 1	4 x (10 x 50 m on 30 sec)	Finish in 6–8 sec	3 min between sets
WEEK 6	Set 1	3 x (10 x 50 m on 30 sec)	Finish in 6–8 sec	3 min between sets

TRAIN TOUGH

Pre-season II (Weeks 7–12)

DAY		DAY		
Monday	Speed / Power	Friday	Strength	
Tuesday		Saturday	Fitness	
Wednesday	Fitness	Sunday		
Thursday				

NB: Each session must be proceeded by 10 min of light aerobic activity and short-duration high-frequency lower limb flexibility, and followed with 20–30 min of medium–long duration, low frequency flexibility.

MONDAY

		WORK	INTENSITY	RECOVERY
WEEK 1	Set 1	4 x 20 m skip into 30 m run (stay tall in skip then into run)	Skip @ 50%, run @ 80%	Walkback recovery on all reps
	Set 2	4 x (5 jumps for distance) 1min rec + 40 m sprint with 'cuts' @ 10 m & 20 m	Jump @ 90%, run @ 100%	
	Set 3	6 x (3 jumps laterally into 30 m sprint with 'cut' at 10 m – do 3 x left, 3 x right)	Jump @ 90%, run @ 100%	3 min between all sets
WEEK 2	Set 1	4 x 20 m skip into 30 m run (stay tall in skip then into run)	Skip @ 50%, run @ 80%	Walkback recovery on all reps
	Set 2	5 x (5 jumps for distance) 1min rec + 40 m sprint with 'cuts' @ 10 m & 20 m	Jump @ 90%, run @ 100%	
	Set 3	6 x (4 jumps laterally into 30 m sprint with 'cut' at 10 m – do 3 x left, 3 x right)	Jump @ 90%, run @ 100%	3 min between all sets
WEEK 3	Set 1	3 x 20 m skip into 30 m run (stay tall in skip then into run)	Skip @ 50%, run @ 80 %	Walkback recovery on all reps
	Set 2	3 x (5 jumps for distance) 1min recovery + 40 m sprint with 'cuts' @ 10 m & 20 m	Jump @ 90%, run @ 100%	
	Set 3	4 x (4 jumps laterally into 30 m sprint with 'cut' at 10 m – do 3 x left, 3 x right)	Jump @ 90%, run @ 100%	3 min between all sets

MONDAY (cont.)

		WORK	INTENSITY	RECOVERY
WEEK 4	Set 1	3 x 30 m skip into 30 m run	Skip @ 75%, run @ 80%	Walkback recovery
	Set 2	4 x (4 x one clap push up + 30 m sprint with 'cuts' at 10 m & 20 m)	Explosive push ups Sprint @ 100%	Walkback recovery
	Set 3	6 x sprint 10 m 'turn & go' 30 m in opposite direction	100%	Walkback recovery
WEEK 5	Set 1	3 x 30 m skip into 30 m run	Skip @ 75%, run @ 80%	Walkback recovery
	Set 2	5 x (4 x one clap push up + 30 m sprint with 'cuts' at 10 m & 20 m)	Explosive push ups Sprint @ 100%	Walkback recovery
	Set 3	6 x sprint 20 m 'turn & go' 30 m in opposite direction	100%	Walkback recovery
WEEK 6	Set 1	2 x 30 m skip into 30 m run	Skip @ 75%, run @ 80%	Walkback recovery
	Set 2	3 x (4 x one clap push up + 30 m sprint with 'cuts' at 10 m & 20 m)	Explosive push ups Sprint @ 100%	Walkback recovery
	Set 3	3 x sprint 20 m 'turn & go' 30 m in opposite direction	100%	Walkback recovery

TRAIN TOUGH

WEDNESDAY

		WORK	INTENSITY	RECOVERY
WEEK 1	Set 1	3 x (4 x 120 m)	Finish in 20–24 sec	30 sec btwn reps 3 min btwn sets
WEEK 2	Set 1	4 x (4 x 120 m)	Finish in 20–24 sec	30 sec btw reps 3 min btw sets
WEEK 3	Set 1	4 x (4 x 120 m)	Finish in 20–24 sec	30 sec btw reps 3 min btw sets
WEEK 4	Set 1	4 x 60 m – Tempo runs	80% effort – focus on rhythm!	Walk back between each rep. 3 min rest before Set 2
	Set 2	8 x 40 m – Speed	100%	3 min between each rep
WEEK 5	Set 1	3 x 60 m – Tempo runs	80% effort – focus on rhythm!	Walk back between each rep. 3 min rest before Set 2
	Set 2	4 x 40 m – Speed	100%	3 min between each rep
	Set 3	6 x 30 m – Speed	100%	3 min between each rep
WEEK 6	Set 1	4 x 50 m – Tempo runs	80% effort – focus on rhythm!	Walk back between each rep. 3 min rest before Set 2
	Set 2	3 x 40 m – Speed	100%	2 min between each rep
	Set 3	4 x 30 m – Speed	100%	2 min between each rep

FRIDAY

ORDER	EXERCISE	TEMPO	REC	WEEK 1	WEEK 2	WEEK 3	WEEK 4	WEEK 5	WEEK 6
A	**Squat**	3/1/1	2 min	3 x 6	N/A	3 x 6	N/A	3 x 6	N/A
A (alt)	**Power Squat** (use 75% of the weight used the previous week)	3/0/X Max Speed	1 min	N/A	8 x 3	N/A	8 x 3	N/A	8 x 3
B	Good Morning	4/1/1	2 min	3 x 6	3 x 4	2 x 6	3 x 4	3 x 6	2 x 4
C	UG Chin-ups	3/1/1	90 sec	4 x 6	4 x 4	2 x 6	4 x 4	4 x 6	2 x 4
D	**Bench Press**	2/1/1	2 min	3 x 6	N/A	3 x 6	N/A	3 x 6	N/A
D (alt)	**Power Bench Press** (use 75% of the weight used the previous week)	2/0/X Max Speed	1 min	N/A	8 x 3	N/A	8 x 3	N/A	8 x 3
E	Dips (add weight)	3/1/1	90 sec	3 x 6	3 x 4	2 x 6	3 x 4	3 x 6	2 x 4

NB:
- Exercises in **bold** are alternated every second week.
- Power Squat and Bench Press are categorised by controlled lowering of the weight and application of maximum speed to the bar from the bottom position.

SATURDAY

		WORK	INTENSITY	RECOVERY
WEEK 1	SET 1	6 x 2 min (measure distance – try to maintain for each rep)	Zone 3 (85–90% MHR)	3 min between reps
WEEK 2	SET 1	6 x 2 min (measure distance – try to beat best result from previous week)	Zone 3	3 min between reps
WEEK 3	SET 1	4 x 2 min (measure distance – try to beat best result from previous week)	Zone 3	3 min between reps
WEEK 4	Set 1	3 x (10 x 100 m on 50 sec)	Finish in 14–16 sec	3 min between sets
WEEK 5	Set 1	4 x (10 x 50 m on 25 sec)	Finish in 6–8 sec	3 min between sets
WEEK 6	Set 1	3 x (10 x 50 m on 25 sec)	Finish in 6–8 sec	3 min between sets

TRAIN TOUGH

IN-SEASON TRAINING

The trick with in-season training is to always balance your physical preparation with the training requirements of the team. The number of games per week plus team training (not to mention family and social commitments) will dictate the amount of time you can commit to individual preparation.

The main focus of the in-season period is to retain the improvements in physical performance that have been achieved during the pre-season while remaining as fresh as possible for games. The rate at which a performance variable decays (gets worse following the stopping of training) will dictate how frequently you need to train that variable. For example:

■ **Speed** is basically a function of neuromuscular drive (power) and coordination (running skills). Power elements are best addressed every 7–10 days. Low volume is generally required to maintain performance levels so power elements may be included in a session with other variables such as lactate tolerance running. Speed skills (running coordination) are best addressed every 3–4 days particularly in lesser-trained individuals. This may simply take the form of several tempo runs (as described on p 154) in the latter stages of your warm up.

Estimating speed performance

Without using timing lights or other specialist equipment you can keep track of your speed performance with a stop watch, two markers and a friend with good hand–eye coordination.

■ Mark out the distance you want to measure – standard in many field sports is 40 m.

■ Have your timer stand with the stop watch at the finish line (you stand at the start).

■ Signal your partner when you are ready to go (after a thorough warm up and several run throughs).

■ Your timer must start the watch when your first foot hits the ground (not when your foot is lifted).

■ The watch is then stopped when your chest passes the finish line.

■ Use the average of 3–4 attempts as representative of your speed at that time.

NB: As with everything in sports, many coaches have their own variation on the above technique. The important thing to remember is to use the same method every time, with the same person timing you, and you should get some reliability in your data collection.

- **Strength:** Depending on the degree to which strength is important in your sport, this variable may be addressed every week or as infrequently as once every two weeks. Training age plays a large part in the retention of strength gains. The more experienced an athlete is, the more strength will be retained.

- **Running fitness:** To simplify this area, you need to consider two components of running fitness.

  1 **Aerobic Capacities:** 'Long time gained, long time lost.' Broadly speaking, adaptations that take a significant amount of time to achieve are slow to detrain. The greater the training age of the athlete the more this holds true. The same applies for those of limited training age – adaptations that have not been sustained for a significant period will detrain rapidly. In the latter case, aerobic capacities would need to be addressed every 12–15 days.

  2 **Anaerobic capacities:** These performance parameters take between 3–4 weeks to peak in most athletes and then need to be addressed every 7–10 days to maintain optimal performance.

The key to maintenance of all performance variables is the retention of *intensity* in training. *Volume* may be reduced by as much as 60 per cent in some cases, but *intensity* must be retained at close to 100 per cent for performance to be retained.

IMPORTANT:
TRAINING AT A REDUCED VOLUME WILL ONLY SUCCEED IN RETAINING YOUR PERFORMANCE LEVELS FOR A FINITE PERIOD OF TIME. IN THE CASE OF A LONG SEASON – ANY FOOTBALL CODE – IT MAY BE NECESSARY TO APPLY GREATER VOLUME STIMULUS AT PERIODS THROUGHOUT THE SEASON. OFTEN THIS IS DONE DURING A BYE OR IN THE LEAD-UP TO WHAT YOU CONSIDER A LESSER GAME.

13 MUSCLE UP

At some point in most guys' lives they're struck by the desire to 'get massive'. While the aim might be simple, the path can be somewhat difficult. That's why this section has a number of options for rapidly achieving increased muscularity. But let's not dispense words. Let's just get on with it and lift hard!

VARIETY

Without question, it's in the realm of mass muscle production that the principle of variety is most often shunned – particularly by less experienced lifters. It's not sufficient to spend the majority of every session doing bicep curls and bench press. Constant evolution of your program will bring about the greatest and most sustained results.

FREQUENCY

Obviously the more time you have to commit to your 'project' the better and quicker you're going to progress. Unfortunately, the demands of work, family and trying to catch your football team decrees there's a time limit to what you can commit to. Therefore, one of the most critical logistical elements is the number of days per week you can train.

Most of the programs in this section are based around one hour's training, 3–4 days per week. These programs are optimised for this level of frequency. Should you find yourself only able to complete two, sometimes three sessions a week, ensure that you get the first two sessions in as close to the timeframe indicated as possible.

Then, if time permits, grab the third. If you can't get the third session in more than 75 per cent of the time, then re-evaluate your goals to allow for longer time for you to adapt to training.

THREE-DAY PROGRAMS

These programs suit the guys with a bit on their plate, cramming as much training into the week as possible.

Hypertrophy Basic

Prerequisites: minimum 8 weeks, general strength training. (Don't have that? See 'Getting Out of the Blocks' on p 142).

Synopsis: Addresses all body parts 3 times per week. Good starter's program as loads are reasonably low and recovery can be achieved between sessions. 'Wave-Load' allows for alternating increases in intensity.

Day 1 (MONDAY)

ORDER	EXERCISE	TEMPO	REC	WEEK 1	WEEK 2	WEEK 3	WEEK 4
A	Squat	3/2/1	90 sec	3 x 12	3 x 8	3 x 10	3 x 6
B	Good Morning	2/2/2	90 sec	3 x 12	3 x 8	3 x 10	3 x 6
C	Single Leg Bridge	2/2/2	90 sec	3 x 12	3 x 8	3 x 10	3 x 6
D	Pulldowns OH F	3/2/1	90 sec	3 x 12	3 x 8	3 x 10	3 x 6
E	DB Shoulder Press	3/2/1	90 sec	3 x 12	3 x 8	3 x 10	3 x 6
F	Upright Row	2/1/1	90 sec	3 x 12	3 x 8	3 x 10	3 x 6

Day 2 (WEDNESDAY)

ORDER	EXERCISE	TEMPO	REC	WEEK 1	WEEK 2	WEEK 3	WEEK 4
A	Deadlift	3/2/1	90 sec	3 x 12	3 x 8	3 x 10	3 x 6
B	Back Extension	2/2/2	90 sec	3 x 12	3 x 8	3 x 10	3 x 6
C	Single Leg Bridge	2/2/2	90 sec	3 x 12	3 x 8	3 x 10	3 x 6
D	Pulldowns OH F	3/2/1	90 sec	3 x 12	3 x 8	3 x 10	3 x 6
E	DB Shoulder Press	3/2/1	90 sec	3 x 12	3 x 8	3 x 10	3 x 6
F	Upright Row	2/1/1	90 sec	3 x 12	3 x 8	3 x 10	3 x 6

Day 3 (FRIDAY)

ORDER	EXERCISE	TEMPO	REC	WEEK 1	WEEK 2	WEEK 3	WEEK 4
A	Front Squat	3/2/1	90 sec	3 x 12	3 x 8	3 x 10	3 x 6
B	Back Extension	2/2/2	90 sec	3 x 12	3 x 8	3 x 10	3 x 6
C	Single Leg Bridge	2/2/2	90 sec	3 x 12	3 x 8	3 x 10	3 x 6
D	Pulldowns OH F	3/2/1	90 sec	3 x 12	3 x 8	3 x 10	3 x 6
E	DB Shoulder Press	3/2/1	90 sec	3 x 12	3 x 8	3 x 10	3 x 6
F	Upright Row	2/1/1	90 sec	3 x 12	3 x 8	3 x 10	3 x 6

Rotation Hypertrophy Basic

Prerequisites: minimum 8 weeks, general strength training (See 'Getting Out of the Blocks' on p 142) or Basic Hypertrophy on p 170.

Synopsis: Addresses all body parts 3 times per week, but places specific emphasis on one upper body part per day (highlighted). Overall loads are low-moderate and therefore recovery can be achieved between sessions but extra attention must be paid to nutrition and sleep. 'Wave-Load' allows for alternating increases in intensity. Note use of Tri-Sets, Pre-Exhaustion Sets and Super-Sets (indicated by letter combinations in 'order' column).

CHEAT NOTES

- **Tri-set:** Series of three exercises in succession, usually aimed at achieving broad range fatigue in one muscle group.

- **Pre-exhaustion set:** Series of two exercises utilising the same body part aimed at increasing fatigue in the targeted muscle group.

- **Super set:** Series of two exercises incorporating opposing muscle groups aimed at increasing session density (exercises per minute) and utilising reciprocal inhibition (as one muscle group fatigues the opposite relaxes and is primed for performance).

- **Highlighted exercises:** Indicate the focus muscle groups in each session.

Day 1 (MONDAY)

ORDER	EXERCISE	TEMPO	REC	WEEK 1	WEEK 2	WEEK 3	WEEK 4
A	Front Squat	3/2/1	90 sec	3 x 12	3 x 8	3 x 10	3 x 6
B	Deadlift	2/2/2	90 sec	3 x 12	3 x 8	3 x 10	3 x 6
C	Good Morning	2/2/2	90 sec	3 x 12	3 x 8	3 x 10	3 x 6
D1	Military Press	3/2/1	N/A	3 x 8	3 x 8	3 x 8	3 x 8
D2	DB Shoulder Press	3/2/1	N/A	3 x 12	3 x 12	3 x 12	3 x 12
D3	Upright Row	2/0/1	90 sec	3 x 12	3 x 12	3 x 12	3 x 12
E1	Chin-ups UG	3/1/1	N/A	3 x 12	3 x 8	3 x 10	3 x 6
E2	DB Hammer Curl	3/2/1	90 sec	3 x 12	3 x 8	3 x 10	3 x 6

Day 2 (WEDNESDAY)

ORDER	EXERCISE	TEMPO	REC	WEEK 1	WEEK 2	WEEK 3	WEEK 4
A	Deadlift	3/2/1	90 sec	3 x 12	3 x 8	3 x 10	3 x 6
B	Front Squat	2/2/2	90 sec	3 x 12	3 x 8	3 x 10	3 x 6
C	DB Romanian Deadlift	2/2/2	90 sec	3 x 12	3 x 8	3 x 10	3 x 6
D	Chin-ups UG	3/1/1	90 sec	3 x 8	3 x 10	3 x 12	3 x 12
E1	Pulldowns OH F	3/2/1	N/A	3 x 12	3 x 8	3 x 10	3 x 6
E2	Bent Over Row OH	3/2/1	90 sec	3 x 12	3 x 8	3 x 10	3 x 6
F1	Dips	3/2/1	N/A	3 x 12	3 x 8	3 x 10	3 x 6
F2	EZY Bar Curl	3/2/1	90 sec	3 x 12	3 x 8	3 x 10	3 x 6

Day 3 (FRIDAY)

ORDER	EXERCISE	TEMPO	REC	WEEK 1	WEEK 2	WEEK 3	WEEK 4
A	Squat	3/2/1	90 sec	3 x 12	3 x 8	3 x 10	3 x 6
B	Romanian Deadlift	2/2/2	90 sec	3 x 12	3 x 8	3 x 10	3 x 6
C	Reverse Hyperextensions	2/2/2	90 sec	3 x 8	3 x 10	3 x 12	3 x 12
D1	Wide Grip Bench Press	3/2/1	N/A	3 x 12	3 x 8	3 x 10	3 x 6
D2	Incline DB Press	3/2/1	90 sec	3 x 12	3 x 8	3 x 10	3 x 6
E	Single Arm Row	3/2/1	90 sec	3 x 12	3 x 8	3 x 10	3 x 6
F1	Reverse Curls	3/2/1	N/A	3 x 12	3 x 8	3 x 10	3 x 6
F2	CG Bench Press	3/2/1	90 sec	3 x 12	3 x 8	3 x 10	3 x 6

TRAIN TOUGH

Super Slow

Prerequisites: minimum 8 weeks, general strength training (See 'Getting Out of the Blocks' on p 142) or Basic Hypertrophy on p 170.

Synopsis: Uses *slow* eccentric contractions (lowering component) in the tempo of highlighted exercises to overload muscle fibres via increased time under tension; see Chapter 6, 'Force', for details (very effective). Training intensity must still be maintained as high as possible (use the greatest weight possible while still maintaining technique.) Addresses all body parts 3 times per week. Overall loads are low to moderate and therefore recovery can be achieved between sessions but extra attention must be paid to nutrition and sleep. Wave-Load allows for alternating increases in intensity. *Be disciplined in maintaining the tempo of the lifts.* Fantastic grounding for technique before moving on to more intense programs.

CHEAT NOTES:
Highlighted exercises: Indicates the targeted SLOW tempo lifts.

Day 1 (MONDAY)

ORDER	EXERCISE	TEMPO	REC	WEEK 1	WEEK 2	WEEK 3	WEEK 4
A	Front Squat 1&1/2	2/2/2	90 sec	3 x 10	3 x 6	3 x 8	3 x 4
B	Deadlift	2/2/2	90 sec	3 x 12	3 x 8	3 x 10	3 x 4
C	Good Morning	2/2/2	90 sec	3 x 12	3 x 8	3 x 10	3 x 4
D	Chin-ups OH F	5/1/1	N/A	3 x 4	3 x 6	3 x 8	2 x 8
E	Military Press	4/2/1	90 sec	3 x 8	3 x 6	3 x 8	3 x 4
F	DB Shoulder Press	4/2/1	90 sec	3 x 8	3 x 6	3 x 8	3 x 4
G1	EZY Bar Curl	5/1/1	N/A	3 x 8	3 x 6	3 x 8	3 x 4
G2	DB Hammer Curl	3/2/1	90 sec	3 x 12	3 x 8	3 x 10	3 x 6

Day 2 (WEDNESDAY)

ORDER	EXERCISE	TEMPO	REC	WEEK 1	WEEK 2	WEEK 3	WEEK 4
A	Deadlift	4/1/1	90 sec	3 x 8	3 x 6	3 x 8	3 x 4
B	Reverse Hyperextension	2/2/2	90 sec	3 x 12	3 x 8	3 x 10	3 x 6
C	Supine TB Curl	2/2/2	90 sec	3 x 10	3 x 12	3 x 15	2 x 15
D1	Bent Over Row UH	3/2/1	N/A	3 x 12	3 x 8	3 x 10	3 x 6
D2	Seated Row	4/2/1	90 sec	3 x 8	3 x 6	3 x 8	3 x 4
E	Single Arm Row	3/2/1	90 sec	3 x 12	3 x 8	3 x 10	3 x 6
F1	Dips	5/1/1	N/A	3 x 8	3 x 6	3 x 8	3 x 4
F2	CG Bench Press	3/2/1	90 sec	3 x 12	3 x 8	3 x 10	3 x 6

Day 3 (FRIDAY)

ORDER	EXERCISE	TEMPO	REC	WEEK 1	WEEK 2	WEEK 3	WEEK 4
A	Squat	6/1/1	90 sec	3 x 8	3 x 6	3 x 8	3 x 4
B	Romanian Deadlift	2/2/2	90 sec	3 x 12	3 x 8	3 x 10	3 x 6
C	Supine TB Curl	2/2/2	90 sec	3 x 10	3 x 12	3 x 15	2 x 15
D1	Chin-ups OH F	5/1/1	N/A	3 x 4	3 x 6	3 x 8	3 x 6
D2	Bench Press	4/2/1	90 sec	3 x 8	3 x 6	3 x 8	3 x 4
E	Upright Row	2/0/1	90 sec	3 x 12	3 x 8	3 x 10	3 x 6
F1	Dips	5/1/1	N/A	3 x 8	3 x 6	3 x 8	3 x 4
F2	EZY Bar Curl	3/2/1	90 sec	3 x 12	3 x 8	3 x 10	3 x 6

NB:
Stick to the exercise tempos strictly to get the most out of the session.

TRAIN TOUGH

FOUR-DAY PROGRAMS

These programs are designed with the more time-committed lifter in mind. Design is predominantly based around the 2 day split system (Monday, Tuesday plus Thursday, Friday) with a multiple of variants added to that theme.

Basic Hypertrophy

Prerequisites: minimum 8 weeks, general strength training (See 'Getting Out of the Blocks' on p 142).

Synopsis: Uses an alternating lower/upper body pattern. Allows greater emphasis to be placed on the lower body than in some other formats. Wave-Load allows for alternating increases in load.

Day 1 (MONDAY)

ORDER	EXERCISE	TEMPO	REC	WEEK 1	WEEK 2	WEEK 3	WEEK 4
A	Squat	3/1/1	90 sec	4 x 12	4 x 10	4 x 8	2 x 6
B	Deadlift	3/1/1	90 sec	3 x 12	3 x 10	3 x 8	2 x 6
C	Good Morning	4/1/1	90 sec	4 x 12	4 x 10	4 x 8	2 x 6
D	Split Squat	3/1/1	90 sec	3 x 12	3 x 10	3 x 8	2 x 6
E	Single Leg Calf Raise	2/2/2	90 sec	3 x 10	3 x 12	3 x 15	2 x 15

Day 2 (TUESDAY)

ORDER	EXERCISE	TEMPO	REC	WEEK 1	WEEK 2	WEEK 3	WEEK 4
A	Bench Press	3/2/1	90 sec	4 x 12	4 x 8	4 x 10	2 x 6
B1	DB Shoulder Press	3/1/1	N/A	3 x 12	3 x 8	3 x 10	2 x 6
B2	Upright Row	2/0/1	90 sec	3 x 12	3 x 8	3 x 10	2 x 6
C	Chin-ups UG	4/1/1	90 sec	3 x 6	3 x 8	3 x 8	2 x 10
D	Seated Row	3/2/1	90 sec	3 x 12	3 x 8	3 x 10	2 x 6
E1	EZY Bar Curl	3/2/1	N/A	3 x 12	3 x 8	3 x 10	2 x 6
E2	Dips	3/2/1	90 sec	3 x 12	3 x 8	3 x 10	2 x 6

Day 3 (THURSDAY)

ORDER	EXERCISE	TEMPO	REC	WEEK 1	WEEK 2	WEEK 3	WEEK 4
A	Deadlift	3/1/1	90 sec	4 x 8	4 x 6	4 x 8	2 x 4
B	Front Squat 1 1/2	2/2/2	90 sec	3 x 8	3 x 6	3 x 8	2 x 4
C	Good Morning	3/1/1	90 sec	3 x 12	3 x 8	3 x 10	2 x 6
D	Walking Lunge	2/2/1	90 sec	3 x 12 each leg	3 x 8 each leg	3 x 10 each leg	2 x 6 each leg
E	DB Single Leg Calf Raise	2/2/2	90 sec	3 x 12	3 x 10	3 x 8	2 x 10

NB:
Front Squat 1½, see p 50.

Day 4 (FRIDAY)

ORDER	EXERCISE	TEMPO	REC	WEEK 1	WEEK 2	WEEK 3	WEEK 4
A	Chin-ups OH F	3/2/1	90 sec	3 x 6	3 x 8	3 x 8	2 x 10
B1	Bent Over Row UG	3/1/1	N/A	3 x 12	3 x 8	3 x 10	2 x 6
B2	Reverse DB Flys	2/0/1	90 sec	3 x 12	3 x 8	3 x 10	2 x 6
C	Behind Neck Press	4/1/1	90 sec	3 x 10	3 x 8	3 x 10	2 x 6
D	Incline Bench Press	3/2/1	90 sec	3 x 12	3 x 8	3 x 10	2 x 6
E1	DB Hammer Curl	3/2/1	N/A	3 x 12	3 x 8	3 x 10	2 x 6
E2	CG Bench Press	3/2/1	90 sec	3 x 12	3 x 8	3 x 10	2 x 6

TRAIN TOUGH

Super Slow

Prerequisites: Basic Hypertrophy (4 days).

Synopsis: Uses an alternating lower/upper body pattern with the main variant being the use of slow eccentric contractions (lowering component – see notes for 3 day *Super Slow* on p 168). Allows greater emphasis to be placed on the lower body than in some other formats. Wave-Load allows for alternating increases in load.

CHEAT NOTES:
Highlighted exercises: Indicate *super slow* tempo execution.

Remember, exercises listed under the same letter, for example, A1, A2 are completed in succession with no recovery between.

Day 1 (MONDAY)

ORDER	EXERCISE	TEMPO	REC	WEEK 1	WEEK 2	WEEK 3	WEEK 4
A	Squat	5/1/1	90 sec	4 x 8	4 x 6	4 x 8	2 x 6
B	Deadlift	3/1/1	90 sec	3 x 8	3 x 6	3 x 8	2 x 6
C	Good Morning	4/1/1	90 sec	3 x 8	3 x 6	3 x 8	2 x 6
D	Split Squat	5/1/1	90 sec	4 x 8	4 x 6	4 x 8	2 x 6
E	Single Leg Calf Raise	2/2/2	90 sec	3 x 10	3 x 12	3 x 15	2 x 15

Day 2 (TUESDAY)

ORDER	EXERCISE	TEMPO	REC	WEEK 1	WEEK 2	WEEK 3	WEEK 4
A	Bench Press	5/1/1	90 sec	4 x 8	4 x 6	4 x 8	2 x 4
B1	DB Shoulder Press	5/1/1	N/A	4 x 8	4 x 6	4 x 8	2 x 4
B2	Upright Row	2/0/1	90 sec	3 x 12	3 x 8	3 x 10	2 x 6
C	Chin-ups UG	6/1/1	90 sec	3 x 3	3 x 5	3 x 7	2 x 7
D	Seated Row	3/2/1	90 sec	3 x 12	3 x 8	3 x 10	2 x 6
E1	EZY Bar Curl	4/1/1	N/A	3 x 8	3 x 6	3 x 8	2 x 6
E2	Dips	4/1/1	90 sec	3 x 8	3 x 6	3 x 8	2 x 6

Day 3 (THURSDAY)

ORDER	EXERCISE	TEMPO	REC	WEEK 1	WEEK 2	WEEK 3	WEEK 4
A	Deadlift	3/1/1	90 sec	3 x 8	3 x 6	3 x 8	2 x 6
B	Front Squat 1 1/2	3/3/3	90 sec	3 x 4	3 x 6	3 x 4	2 x 6
C	Good Morning	3/1/1	90 sec	3 x 8	3 x 6	3 x 8	2 x 6
D	Walking Lunge	4/2/1	90 sec	3 x 8 each leg	3 x 6 each leg	3 x 8 each leg	2 x 6 each leg
E	DB Single Leg Calf Raise	2/2/2	90 sec	3 x 12	3 x 10	3 x 8	2 x 8

Day 4 (FRIDAY)

ORDER	EXERCISE	TEMPO	REC	WEEK 1	WEEK 2	WEEK 3	WEEK 4
A	Chin-ups OH F	3/2/1	90 sec	3 x 6	3 x 8	3 x 8	2 x 10
B1	Bent Over Row UG	5/1/1	N/A	3 x 8	3 x 6	3 x 8	2 x 6
B2	Reverse DB Flys	2/0/1	90 sec	3 x 12	3 x 8	3 x 10	2 x 8
C	Behind Neck Press	4/2/1	90 sec	3 x 8	3 x 6	3 x 8	2 x 6
D	Incline Bench Press	4/2/1	90 sec	3 x 8	3 x 6	3 x 8	2 x 6
E1	DB Hammer Curl	3/2/1	N/A	3 x 12	3 x 8	3 x 10	2 x 8
E2	CG Bench Press	4/2/1	90 sec	3 x 8	3 x 6	3 x 8	2 x 6

TRAIN TOUGH

Accumulation

Prerequisites: Basic Hypertrophy (3–4 days).
(See 'Getting Out of the Blocks' on p 142).

Synopsis: Traditional 2-Day split system aimed at increasing the total volume of training over the course of the program without significantly increasing the intensity of the weight lifted in core lifts. Precursor to Intensification program.

Day 1 (MONDAY)

ORDER	EXERCISE	TEMPO	REC	WEEK 1	WEEK 2	WEEK 3	WEEK 4
A	Squat	3/1/1	90 sec	6 x 4	5 x 5	4 x 6	3 x 7
B	Split Squat	3/1/1	90 sec	2 x 6	2 x 6	2 x 8	2 x 8
C	Romanian Deadlift	4/1/1	90 sec	6 x 4	5 x 5	4 x 6	3 x 7
D	Incline Bench Press	3/1/1	90 sec	6 x 4	5 x 5	4 x 6	3 x 7
E	Close Grip Bench Press	3/1/1	90 sec	2 x 6	2 x 6	2 x 8	2 x 8
F	Dips	2/1/1	90 sec	2 x 6	2 x 6	2 x 8	2 x 8

NB:
The objective of each set is to select a weight that will allow you to complete the set with perfect technique, yet be fatigued at the completion. In the subsequent weeks the same weight should be used with the increase in the repetition number or density providing the overload.

Day 2 (TUESDAY)

ORDER	EXERCISE	TEMPO	REC	WEEK 1	WEEK 2	WEEK 3	WEEK 4
A	Wide Grip Shrug	2/2/2	90 sec	3 x 8	3 x 9	3 x 10	3 x 12
B1	Behind Neck Press	3/1/1	N/A	3 x 6	3 x 6	3 x 8	3 x 8
B2	Upright Row	2/0/1	90 sec	3 x 6	3 x 6	3 x 8	3 x 8
C	Chin-ups UG	2/1/1	90 sec	6 x 4	5 x 5	4 x 6	3 x 7
D	Bent Over Row OH	3/2/1	90 sec	3 x 8	3 x 9	3 x 10	3 x 12
E	EZY Bar Curl	3/2/1	N/A	3 x 6	3 x 6	3 x 8	3 x 8

Day 3 (THURSDAY)

ORDER	EXERCISE	TEMPO	REC	WEEK 1	WEEK 2	WEEK 3	WEEK 4
A	Deadlift	3/1/1	2 min	6 x 4	5 x 5	4 x 6	3 x 7
B	Front Squat 1 1/2	2/2/2	90 sec	2 x 6	2 x 6	2 x 8	2 x 8
C	Good Morning	3/1/1	90 sec	3 x 6	3 x 6	3 x 8	3 x 8
D	Bench Press	3/1/1	2 min	6 x 4	5 x 5	4 x 6	3 x 7
E	DB Decline Press	3/1/1	90 sec	3 x 6	3 x 6	3 x 8	3 x 8
F	Overhead Cable Tricep Ext.	2/1/1	90 sec	3 x 6	3 x 6	3 x 8	3 x 8

Day 4 (FRIDAY)

ORDER	EXERCISE	TEMPO	REC	WEEK 1	WEEK 2	WEEK 3	WEEK 4
A	Chin-ups OG	2/1/1	90 sec	6 x 4	5 x 5	4 x 6	3 x 7
B1	Seated Row	3/1/1	N/A	3 x 6	3 x 6	3 x 8	3 x 8
B2	Reverse DB Flys	2/0/1	90 sec	3 x 8	3 x 8	3 x 10	3 x 10
C	Military Press	4/1/1	90 sec	6 x 4	5 x 5	4 x 6	3 x 7
D	DB Hammer Curl	3/2/1	90 sec	3 x 6	3 x 6	3 x 8	3 x 8
E1	SLOW DB Curl	5/1/1	N/A	3 x 6	3 x 6	3 x 8	3 x 8
E2	Cable Curl	2/1/1	90 sec	3 x 6	3 x 6	3 x 8	3 x 8

TRAIN TOUGH

Intensification

Prerequisites: Basic Hypertrophy (4 days), Super Slow (4 days) or Accumulation (4 days).

Synopsis: Traditional 2-Day split system (reduced volume on lower body to accommodate higher intensity). Program is aimed at hypertrophy and introductory maximal strength and is suited to the more experienced lifter. Natural succession to the Accumulation program.

Day 1 (MONDAY)

ORDER	EXERCISE	TEMPO	REC	WEEK 1	WEEK 2	WEEK 3	WEEK 4
A	Squat	3/1/1	2 min	8/6/4/4	8/6/4/4	6/4/6/4	6/4/6/4
B	Split Squat	3/1/1	90 sec	2 x 8	2 x 8	2 x 6	2 x 6
C	Romanian Deadlift	4/1/1	2 min	4 x 6	4 x 4	4 x 6	4 x 4
D .	Incline Bench Press	3/1/1	2 min	8/6/4/4	8/6/4/4	6/4/6/4	6/4/6/4
E	Close Grip Bench Press	3/1/1	90 sec	3 x 8	3 x 8	3 x 6	3 x 6
F	Dips	2/1/1	90 sec	3 x 8	3 x 8	3 x 6	3 x 6

NB:
Overload in this program is based on increasing the absolute weight lifted. As reps decrease the weight lifted should be increased.

Day 2 (TUESDAY)

ORDER	EXERCISE	TEMPO	REC	WEEK 1	WEEK 2	WEEK 3	WEEK 4
A	Wide Grip Shrug	2/2/2	90 sec	3 x 8	3 x 8	3 x 6	3 x 6
B1	Behind Neck Press	3/1/1	N/A	3 x 8	3 x 8	3 x 6	3 x 6
B2	Upright Row	2/0/1	90 sec	3 x 8	3 x 8	3 x 6	3 x 6
C	Chin-ups UG	2/1/1	90 sec	8/6/4/4	8/6/4/4	6/4/6/4	6/4/6/4
D	Bent Over Row OH	3/2/1	90 sec	3 x 8	3 x 8	3 x 6	3 x 6
E	EZY Bar Curl	3/2/1	N/A	3 x 8	3 x 8	3 x 6	3 x 6

Day 3 (THURSDAY)

ORDER	EXERCISE	TEMPO	REC	WEEK 1	WEEK 2	WEEK 3	WEEK 4
A	Deadlift	3/1/1	2 min	8/6/4/4	8/6/4/4	6/4/6/4	6/4/6/4
B	Front Squat 1 1/2	2/2/2	90 sec	2 x 8	2 x 8	2 x 6	2 x 6
C	Good Morning	3/1/1	90 sec	4 x 8	4 x 6	4 x 8	4 x 6
D	Bench Press	3/1/1	2 min	8/6/4/4	8/6/4/4	6/4/6/4	6/4/6/4
E	DB Decline Press	3/1/1	90 sec	3 x 8	3 x 8	3 x 6	3 x 6
F	Overhead Cable Tricep Ext.	2/1/1	90 sec	3 x 8	3 x 8	3 x 6	3 x 6

Day 4 (FRIDAY)

ORDER	EXERCISE	TEMPO	REC	WEEK 1	WEEK 2	WEEK 3	WEEK 4
A	Chin-ups OG	2/1/1	90 sec	8/6/4/4	8/6/4/4	6/4/6/4	6/4/6/4
B1	Seated Row	3/1/1	N/A	3 x 8	3 x 8	3 x 6	3 x 6
B2	Reverse DB Flys	2/0/1	90 sec	3 x 10	3 x 10	3 x 8	3 x 8
C	Military Press	4/1/1	90 sec	3 x 10	3 x 10	3 x 8	2 x 8
D	DB Hammer Curl	3/2/1	90 sec	2 x 12	2 x 8	2 x 10	2 x 6
E1	SLOW DB Curl	5/1/1	N/A	3 x 6	3 x 6	3 x 6	3 x 6
E2	Cable Curl	2/1/1	90 sec	3 x 8	3 x 8	3 x 8	3 x 8

TRAIN TOUGH

Slow (beginner) Push Pull
Prerequisites: Basic Hypertrophy (4 days), or Super Slow (4 days).

Synopsis: 2-Day split system, using a push/pull structure. This structure splits lower body lifts into pushing and pulling techniques, then groups them with upper body push/pull movements on the same day. This increases the recovery time between core lifts, therefore reducing residual fatigue in subsequent sessions and allowing for greater application of training intensity (weight). Suited to lifters of moderate experience (1–2 years, experience). Exaggerated eccentric component aimed at increasing time under tension.

Aim of program: Hypertrophy

Day 1 (MONDAY)

ORDER	EXERCISE	TEMPO	REC	WEEK 1	WEEK 2	WEEK 3	WEEK 4
A	Front Squat	6/1/1	90 sec	4 x 8	4 x 6	4 x 8	3 x 6
B	Split Squat	4/2/1	90 sec	3 x 8	3 x 6	3 x 8	3 x 6
C	Single Leg Calf Raise	2/2/2	90 sec	3 x 10	3 x 12	3 x 15	2 x 15
D	DB Bench Press 1&1/2	2/2/2	90 sec	3 x 6	3 x 8	3 x 6	2 x 8
E	Decline Bench Press	5/1/1	90 sec	3 x 8	3 x 6	3 x 8	2 x 6
F	DB Shoulder Press	3/1/1	90 sec	3 x 12	3 x 8	3 x 10	2 x 6
G	Dips	5/1/1	90 sec	3 x 8	3 x 6	3 x 8	2 x 6

Day 2 (TUESDAY)

ORDER	EXERCISE	TEMPO	REC	WEEK 1	WEEK 2	WEEK 3	WEEK 4
A	Deadlift	3/1/1	90 sec	4 x 10	4 x 6	4 x 8	3 x 6
B	Good Morning	5/1/1	90 sec	3 x 8	3 x 6	3 x 8	2 x 6
C	Chin-ups UG 1&1/2	2/2/2	90 sec	3 x 6	3 x 8	3 x 6	2 x 8
D	Single Arm Row	3/2/1	90 sec	3 x 12	3 x 8	3 x 10	2 x 6
E	Upright Row	2/0/1	90 sec	3 x 12	3 x 8	3 x 10	2 x 6
F1	EZY Reverse Curl	4/1/1	N/A	3 x 8	3 x 6	3 x 8	2 x 6
F2	EZY Bar Curl	4/1/1	90 sec	3 x 8	3 x 6	3 x 8	2 x 6

Day 3 (THURSDAY)

ORDER	EXERCISE	TEMPO	REC	WEEK 1	WEEK 2	WEEK 3	WEEK 4
A	Squat	6/1/1	90 sec	3 x 8	3 x 4	3 x 6	2 x 4
B	Walking Lunge	3/1/1	90 sec	3 x 10 each leg	3 x 6 each leg	3 x 8 each leg	2 x 6 each leg
C	DB Single Leg Calf Raise	2/2/2	90 sec	3 x 12	3 x 8	3 x 10	2 x 6
D	Behind Neck Press	5/1/1	90 sec	3 x 8	3 x 4	3 x 6	2 x 4
E	Incline Bench Press	5/1/1	90 sec	3 x 8	3 x 4	3 x 6	2 x 4
F1	Dips	5/1/1	N/A	3 x 8	3 x 6	3 x 8	2 x 6
F2	CG Bench Press	3/1/1	90 sec	3 x 8	3 x 6	3 x 8	2 x 6

Day 4 (FRIDAY)

ORDER	EXERCISE	TEMPO	REC	WEEK 1	WEEK 2	WEEK 3	WEEK 4
A	Romanian Deadlift	6/1/1	90 sec	4 x 6	4 x 8	4 x 6	2 x 4
B	Reverse Hyper Extension/Leg Curl	2/2/2	90 sec	3 x 12	3 x 8	3 x 10	2 x 6
C	Chin-ups OH F	5/1/1	90 sec	3 x 6	3 x 8	3 x 10	2 x 10
D	Pulldowns WG F	4/2/1	90 sec	3 x 8	3 x 6	3 x 8	2 x 6
E	Upright Row	2/0/1	90 sec	3 x 12	3 x 8	3 x 10	2 x 6
F1	DB Hammer Curl	3/1/1	N/A	3 x 12	3 x 8	3 x 10	2 x 6
F2	EZY Bar Curl 1&1/2	2/2/2	90 sec	3 x 6	3 x 8	3 x 6	2 x 8

TRAIN TOUGH

Intermediate Push Pull

Prerequisites: Basic Hypertrophy (4 days), or Super Slow (4 days).

Synopsis: 2-Day split system, using a push/pull structure. Suited to more experienced lifters (2–3 years' experience). Wave-Load used to increase intensity.

Aim of program: Hypertrophy

Day 1 (MONDAY)

ORDER	EXERCISE	TEMPO	REC	WEEK 1	WEEK 2	WEEK 3	WEEK 4
A	Front Squat	3/1/1	90 sec	4 x 12	4 x 8	4 x 10	3 x 6
B	Split Squat	3/1/1	90 sec	2 x 12	2 x 10	2 x 8	2 x 6
C	Single Leg Calf Raise	2/2/2	90 sec	3 x 10	3 x 12	3 x 15	2 x 15
D	Incline Bench Press	3/1/1	90 sec	3 x 10	3 x 6	3 x 8	2 x 6
E	DB Bench Press 1	3/1/1	90 sec	3 x 6	3 x 4	3 x 6	2 x 4
F	DB Shoulder Press	3/1/1	90 sec	3 x 10	3 x 8	3 x 10	2 x 6
G	Dips	3/2/1	90 sec	3 x 10	3 x 8	3 x 10	2 x 6

Day 2 (TUESDAY)

ORDER	EXERCISE	TEMPO	REC	WEEK 1	WEEK 2	WEEK 3	WEEK 4
A	Deadlift	3/1/1	90 sec	4 x 6	4 x 4	4 x 5	4 x 4
B	Reverse Hyper	3/1/1	90 sec	3 x 10	3 x 8	3 x 10	3 x 6
C	Chin-ups MG	3/1/1	90 sec	4 x 8	4 x 6	4 x 8	3 x 4
D	Seated Row	3/2/1	90 sec	3 x 10	3 x 8	3 x 10	2 x 6
E	Upright Row	2/0/1	90 sec	3 x 8	3 x 8	3 x 6	2 x 6
F1	EZY Reverse Curl	3/2/1	N/A	3 x 12	3 x 8	3 x 10	2 x 6
F2	EZY Bar Curl	3/2/1	90 sec	3 x 12	3 x 8	3 x 10	2 x 6

Day 3 (THURSDAY)

ORDER	EXERCISE	TEMPO	REC	WEEK 1	WEEK 2	WEEK 3	WEEK 4
A	Squat	4/2/1	90 sec	4 x 8	4 x 6	4 x 8	3 x 4
B	Walking Lunge	3/1/1	90 sec	3 x 10 each leg	3 x 8 each leg	3 x 6 each leg	2 x 6 each leg
C	DB Single Leg Calf Raise	2/2/2	90 sec	2 x 12	2 x 10	2 x 8	2 x 8
D	DB Shoulder Press 1 1/2	2/2/2	90 sec	3 x 8	3 x 6	3 x 8	2 x 6
E	Bench Press	3/2/1	90 sec	4 x 8	4 x 6	4 x 8	3 x 4
F	Dips 1 1/2	2/2/2	90 sec	3 x 10	3 x 6	3 x 8	2 x 6
G	DB Hammer Press	3/1/1	90 sec	2 x 12	2 x 8	2 x 10	2 x 6

Day 4 (FRIDAY)

ORDER	EXERCISE	TEMPO	REC	WEEK 1	WEEK 2	WEEK 3	WEEK 4
A	Romanian Deadlift	3/1/1	90 sec	4 x 8	4 x 6	4 x 8	3 x 4
B	Reverse Hyper Extension/Leg Curl	2/2/2	90 sec	3 x 8	3 x 6	3 x 8	2 x 6
C	Chin-ups OH F	3/1/1	90 sec	3 x 10	3 x 6	3 x 8	2 x 6
D	Pulldowns WG F	3/1/1	90 sec	2 x 8	2 x 6	2 x 8	2 x 6
E	Upright Row	2/0/1	90 sec	3 x 12	3 x 10	3 x 8	2 x 8
F	EZY Reverse Curl	3/1/1	90 sec	3 x 12	3 x 10	3 x 8	2 x 8
G	EZY Bar Curl	3/1/1	90 sec	3 x 12	3 x 10	3 x 8	2 x 8

TRAIN TOUGH

Advanced Push Pull

Prerequisites: Intermediate Push Pull

Synopsis: Structure of program similar to that of the intermediate form. Should only be completed by experienced lifters (2–3 years' experience).

Aim of program: Advanced hypertrophy/intro maximum strength

NB:
The key to success in this program is intensity, that is, the weight lifted. Recovery periods are longer and the total number of lifts is less – therefore the environment is right to lift heavier. Remember, one of the keys to increased strength and size is mechanical stress (weight lifted). Irrespective of weight, maintain perfect technique at all times. *Never increase weight at the expense of technique!*

Day 1 (MONDAY)

ORDER	EXERCISE	TEMPO	REC	WEEK 1	WEEK 2	WEEK 3	WEEK 4
A	Squat	3/1/1	2–3 min	6/4/6/4	6/2/6/2	6/4/6/4	6/2/6/2
B	Split Squat	3/1/1	2 min	3 x 6	3 x 6	3 x 6	2 x 6
C	Decline Bench Press	2/1/X	2–3 min	6/4/6/4	6/2/6/2	6/4/6/4	6/2/6/2
D	Incline DB Press	2/1/X	2 min	3 x 6	3 x 6	3 x 6	2 x 6
E	DB Shoulder Press	3/1/1	2 min	3 x 6	3 x 6	3 x 6	2 x 6
F	Dips	2/1/1	90 sec	3 x 6	3 x 6	3 x 6	2 x 6

Day 2 (TUESDAY)

ORDER	EXERCISE	TEMPO	REC	WEEK 1	WEEK 2	WEEK 3	WEEK 4
A	Deadlift	0/1/1	2–3 min	6/4/6/4	4/2/4/2	4 x 4	4/2/4/2
B	Good Morning	3/1/1	90 sec	3 x 6	3 x 6	3 x 6	2 x 6
C	Chin-ups OH MG	3/1/1	2 min	6/4/6/4	4 x 6	6/4/6/4	4 x 4
D	Bench Pull/Seated Row	2/1/1	90 sec	3 x 6	3 x 6	3 x 6	2 x 6
E	Upright Row	2/0/1	90 sec	3 x 6	3 x 6	3 x 6	2 x 6
F1	EZY Reverse Curl	3/2/1	N/A	2 x 6	2 x 6	2 x 6	2 x 6
F2	EZY Bar Curl	3/2/1	90 sec	2 x 8	2 x 8	2 x 8	2 x 8

Day 3 (THURSDAY)

ORDER	EXERCISE	TEMPO	REC	WEEK 1	WEEK 2	WEEK 3	WEEK 4
A	Leg Press	3/1/1	2–3 min	6/4/6/4	6/2/6/2	6/4/6/4	6/2/6/2
B	Walking Lunge	3/1/1	90 sec	3 x 6 each leg	3 x 6 each leg	3 x 6 each leg	2 x 6 each leg
C	Squat (ensure full range)	4/2/1	N/A	1 x 12	1 x 12	1 x 12	1 x 12
D	Military Press	2/1/X	2–3 min	6/4/6/4	6/2/6/2	6/4/6/4	6/2/6/2
E	Bench Press	2/1/X	2 min	3 x 6	3 x 6	3 x 6	2 x 6
F	Dips	2/1/1	N/A	1 x max no. (must be over 10 or add 2 x 8 Tri Pushdown)	1 x max no. (must be over 10 or add 2 x 8 Tri Pushdown)	1 x max no. (must be over 10 or add 2 x 8 Tri Pushdown)	1 x max no. (must be over 10 or add 2 x 8 Tri Pushdown)

Day 4 (FRIDAY)

ORDER	EXERCISE	TEMPO	REC	WEEK 1	WEEK 2	WEEK 3	WEEK 4
A	Romanian Deadlift	3/1/1	90 sec	4 x 12	4 x 8	4 x 10	3 x 6
B	Reverse Hyper Extension	2/2/2	90 sec	3 x 12	3 x 8	3 x 10	2 x 6
C	Chin-ups OH F	3/1/1	90 sec	3 x 12	3 x 8	3 x 10	2 x 6
D	Pulldowns WG F	3/1/1	90 sec	3 x 12	3 x 8	3 x 10	2 x 6
E	Upright Row	2/0/1	90 sec	3 x 12	3 x 8	3 x 10	2 x 6
F1	EZY Reverse Curl	3/1/1	90 sec	3 x 12	3 x 8	3 x 10	2 x 6
F2	EZY Bar Curl	3/1/1	90 sec	3 x 12	3 x 8	3 x 10	2 x 6

TRAIN TOUGH

SIX-DAY PROGRAMS

As with the 4-Day programs, this is strictly the dominion of the committed lifter/body builder. These programs are based on 2 times three-day training blocks followed by one day recovery. This system is far more demanding on the body as a whole and as such must be preceded by a minimum of 2–3 years of consistent training. A six-day program may be used over a two-week period simply as a 'shock' technique. Using the six-day program in this fashion may serve to break a plateau in training (given it is followed by an appropriate recovery period).

Advanced 3-Day Split (6 days training)

Prerequisites: Advanced Push Pull, Intensification (4 day)

Synopsis: Program splits lower body, upper body push and upper body pulling movements onto 3 consecutive days, with a day's recovery. And repeat.

Aim of program: Hypertrophy/max strength

Day 1 (MONDAY)

ORDER	EXERCISE	TEMPO	REC	WEEK 1	WEEK 2	WEEK 3	WEEK 4
A	Squat	3/1/1	2–3 min	6/4/6/4	6/2/6/2	6/4/6/4	6/2/6/2
B	Split Squat	3/1/1	2 min	3 x 6	3 x 6	3 x 6	2 x 6
C	Romanian Deadlift	4/1/1	2 min	6/4/6/4	6/4/6/4	6/4/6/4	6/4/6/4
D	Single Leg Bridge (any variation)	2/2/2	90 sec	3 x 12	3 x 12	3 x 15	2 x 15
E	DB Single Leg Calf Raise	2/2/2	90 sec	2 x 12	2 x 10	2 x 8	2 x 8

Day 2 (TUESDAY)

ORDER	EXERCISE	TEMPO	REC	WEEK 1	WEEK 2	WEEK 3	WEEK 4
A	Bench Press	2/1/X	2–3 min	6/4/6/4	6/2/6/2	6/4/6/4	6/2/6/2
B	Decline DB Press	2/1/X	2 min	3 x 6	3 x 6	3 x 6	2 x 6
C	Behind Neck Press	2/1/X	2–3 min	8/6/8/6	6/4/6/4	8/6/8/6	6/4/6/4
D	DB Shoulder Press	2/1/1	90 sec	3 x 6	3 x 6	3 x 6	2 x 6
E	Dips	2/1/1	90 sec	2 x 6	2 x 6	2 x 6	2 x 6
F	OH Cable Ext	2/1/1	90 sec	2 x 8	2 x 8	2 x 8	2 x 8

Day 3 (WEDNESDAY)

ORDER	EXERCISE	TEMPO	REC	WEEK 1	WEEK 2	WEEK 3	WEEK 4
A	Chin-ups UG	3/1/1	2 min	8/6/8/6	6/4/6/4	8/6/8/6	6/4/6/4
B	Seated Row WG	3/2/1	90 sec	3 x 6	3 x 6	3 x 6	2 x 6
C	Wide Grip Shrug	2/2/2	90 sec	8/6/8/6	6/4/6/4	8/6/8/6	6/4/6/4
D	DB Shrugs	2/2/2	90 sec	3 x 6	3 x 6	3 x 6	2 x 6
E1	Reverse Curl	2/1/1	N/A	2 x 8	2 x 6	2 x 8	2 x 6
E2	Hammer Curl	2/1/1	N/A	2 x 8	2 x 6	2 x 8	2 x 6
E3	Standard Curl	2/1/1	90 sec	2 x 8	2 x 6	2 x 8	2 x 6

NB:
Use EZY Bar for set E.

Day 4 (THURSDAY)

ORDER	EXERCISE	TEMPO	REC	WEEK 1	WEEK 2	WEEK 3	WEEK 4
A	Step Ups (reps each leg)	3/1/1	2–3 min	8/6/8/6	6/4/6/4	8/6/8/6	6/4/6/4
B	Leg Press	3/1/1	2 min	3 x 6	3 x 6	3 x 6	2 x 6
C	Good Morning	4/1/1	2 min	8/6/8/6	8/6/8/6	8/6/8/6	8/6/8/6
D	Single Leg Bridge on TB	2/2/2	90 sec	3 x 6	3 x 6	3 x 6	2 x 6
E	DB Single Leg Calf Raise	2/2/2	90 sec	2 x 12	2 x 10	2 x 8	2 x 8

TRAIN TOUGH

Advanced 3-Day Split (continued)

Day 5 (FRIDAY)

ORDER	EXERCISE	TEMPO	REC	WEEK 1	WEEK 2	WEEK 3	WEEK 4
A	Incline Bench Press	2/1/X	2–3 min	8/6/8/6	6/4/6/4	8/6/8/6	6/4/6/4
B	Close Grip Bench Press	2/1/X	2 min	3 x 6	3 x 6	3 x 6	2 x 6
C1	Military Press	3/2/1	N/A	3 x 6	3 x 6	3 x 6	2 x 6
C2	DB Shoulder Press	3/2/1	N/A	3 x 8	3 x 8	3 x 8	2 x 8
C3	Upright Row	2/0/1	90 sec	3 x 12	3 x 12	3 x 12	2 x 12
D	Dips (slow)	5/1/1	90 sec	4 x 6	4 x 6	4 x 6	2 x 6

Day 5 (FRIDAY)

ORDER	EXERCISE	TEMPO	REC	WEEK 1	WEEK 2	WEEK 3	WEEK 4
A	Chin-ups OG W	3/1/1	2 min	8/6/8/6	6/4/6/4	8/6/8/6	6/4/6/4
B	Pulldowns CG	3/2/1	90 sec	3 x 6	3 x 6	3 x 6	2 x 6
C	Bench Pull	2/2/2	90 sec	8/6/8/6	6/4/6/4	8/6/8/6	6/4/6/4
D	DB Shrugs	2/2/2	90 sec	3 x 6	3 x 6	3 x 6	2 x 6
E	Incline DB Curl	3/1/1	90 sec	3 x 8	3 x 6	3 x 8	2 x 6
F	Preacher Curl	4/1/1	90 sec	3 x 6	3 x 8	3 x 6	2 x 8

TRAIN TOUGH

Two Days Maximum Strength/Hypertrophy

Prerequisites: Advanced Push Pull, Intensification (4 day), 2 years' lifting experience.

Synopsis: Maximum strength program for the time challenged individual. Based on a conventional split between a maximum effort session and a repeated effort session (see 'Sealed Section' on p 200 for more info). This program must be preceded by a minimum of 2 years' lifting experience. Suitable for the individual incorporating other training elements (fitness/speed, etc) into their weekly schedule.

Aim of program: Max strength (with hypertrophy under current)

Session 1 (MONDAY)

ORDER	EXERCISE	TEMPO	REC	WEEK 1	WEEK 2	WEEK 3	WEEK 4
A	Squat	2/1/X	3 min	1 x 8 @ 75%	1 x 8 @ 70%	1 x 6 @ 7.5%	1 x 6 @ 77.5%
		2/1/X	3 min	1 x 6 @ 72.5%	1 x 6 @ 70%	1 x 4 @ 80%	1 x 4 @ 82.5%
		2/1/X	4–5 min	1 x 4 @ 77.5%	1 x 4 @ 77.5%	1 x 2 @ 85%	1 x 2 @ 85%
		2/1/X	4–5 min	1 x 4 @ 80%	1 x 4 @ 82.5%	1 x 2 @ 87.5%	1 x 2 @ 90%
B	Good Morning	3/1/1	2 min	3 x 6	3 x 6	3 x 4	2 x 4
C	Reverse Hyperextensions	2/1/1	2 min	2 x 6	2 x 6	2 x 6	2 x 6
D	Incline Bench Press	2/1/X	2 min	3 x 6	3 x 6	3 x 4	2 x 4
E	Bent Over Row	3/1/1	90 sec	3 x 6	3 x 6	3 x 4	2 x 4
F	Dips	3/1/1	90 sec	3 x 6	3 x 6	3 x 6	2 x 6

Session 2 (THURSDAY)

ORDER	EXERCISE	TEMPO	REC	WEEK 1	WEEK 2	WEEK 3	WEEK 4
A	Bench Press	2/1/X	2 min	1 x 8 @ 70%	1 x 8 @ 72.5%	1 x 6 @ 77.5%	1 x 6 @ 80%
		2/1/X	2 min	1 x 6 @ 75%	1 x 6 @ 77.5%	1 x 4 @ 82.5%	1 x 4 @ 85%
		2/1/X	3 min	1 x 4 @ 80%	1 x 4 @ 80%	1 x 2 @ 87.5%	1 x 2 @87.5%
		2/1/X	3 min	1 x 4 @ 82.5%	1 x 4 @ 85%	1 x 2 @ 90%	1 x 2 @ 92.5%
B	Dips	3/1/1	2 min	1 x 8, 1 x 6, 1 x 4	1 x 8, 1 x 6, 1 x 4	1 x 8, 1 x 6, 1 x 4	1 x 8, 1 x 6
C	Chin-ups OH F	3/1/1	2 min	1 x 8, 1 x 6, 1 x 4	1 x 8, 1 x 6, 1 x 4	1 x 8, 1 x 6, 1 x 4	1 x 8, 1 x 6
D	Deadlift	3/1/1	3 min	3 x 6	3 x 6	3 x 6	3 x 6
E	Good Morning	3/1/1	2 min	1 x 8, 1 x 6, 1 x 4	1 x 8, 1 x 6, 1 x 4	1 x 8, 1 x 6, 1 x 4	1 x 8, 1 x 6
F	Glute Ham Raise	3/0/1	2 min	3 x 6	3 x 6	3 x 6	3 x 6

NB:
Dips must have extra load added.

TRAIN TOUGH

Two Days Maximum Strength/Power

Prerequisites: Maximum Strength/Hypertrophy, Advanced Push Pull, Intensification (4 day), 2 years' lifting experience.

Synopsis: Maximum strength program for the time challenged individual looking to add an explosive element to their training. Based on a conventional split between a maximum effort session and a dynamic/plyometric effort session

(see 'Sealed Section' on p 200 for more info). This program must be preceded by a minimum of 2 years lifting experience. Not suitable for anybody with lower limb or back injuries or disabilities. Suitable for individuals incorporating other training elements (fitness/speed etc) into their weekly schedule.

Aim of program: Max strength (power undercurrent)

Session 1 (MONDAY)

ORDER	EXERCISE	TEMPO	REC	WEEK 1	WEEK 2	WEEK 3	WEEK 4
A	Squat	2/1/X	3 min	1 x 8 @ 67.5%	1 x 8 @ 70%	1 x 6 @ 75%	1 x 6 @ 77.5%
		2/1/X	3 min	1 x 6 @ 72.5%	1 x 6 @ 70%	1 x 4 @ 80%	1 x 4 @ 82.5%
		2/1/X	4–5 min	1 x 4 @ 77.5%	1 x 4 @ 77.5%	1 x 2 @ 85%	1 x 2 @ 85%
		2/1/X	4–5 min	1 x 4 @ 80%	1 x 4 @ 82.5%	1 x 2 @ 87.5%	1 x 2 @ 90%
B	Good Morning	3/1/1	2 min	3 x 6	3 x 6	3 x 4	2 x 4
C	Reverse Hyperextensions	2/1/1	2 min	2 x 6	2 x 6	2 x 6	2 x 6
D	Depth Drop Push Ups	Explosive	3 min	3 x 6 (try 2 plates)	3 x 6	3 x 4 (try 3 plates)	2 x 4
E	Bent Over Row	3/1/1	90 sec	3 x 6	3 x 6	3 x 4	2 x 4
F	Dips	3/1/1	90 sec	3 x 6	3 x 6	3 x 6	2 x 6

NB:
Depth Drop Push-ups should be started using no more than 2 plates (as per picture and description on p 81). In the third week of the program increase the drop height to 3 plates and reduce the reps to 4. Should be conducted on a forgiving surface such as a gym mat.

Session 2 (THURSDAY)

ORDER	EXERCISE	TEMPO	REC	WEEK 1	WEEK 2	WEEK 3	WEEK 4
A	Bench Press	2/1/X	2 min	1 x 8 @ 70%	1 x 8 @ 72.5%	1 x 6 @ 77.5%	1 x 6 @ 80%
		2/1/X	2 min	1 x 6 @ 75%	1 x 6 @ 77.5%	1 x 4 @ 82.5%	1 x 4 @ 85%
		2/1/X	3 min	1 x 4 @ 80%	1 x 4 @ 80%	1 x 2 @ 87.5%	1 x 2 @87.5%
		2/1/X	3 min	1 x 4 @ 82.5%	1 x 4 @ 85%	1 x 2 @ 90%	1 x 2 @92.5%
B	Dips	3/1/1	2 min	1 x 8, 1 x 6, 1 x 4	1 x 8, 1 x 6, 1 x 4	1 x 8, 1 x 6, 1 x 4	1 x 8, 1 x 6
C	Chin-ups OH F	3/1/1	2 min	1 x 8, 1 x 6, 1 x 4	1 x 8, 1 x 6, 1 x 4	1 x 8, 1 x 6, 1 x 4	1 x 8, 1 x 6
D	Borzov Jump	Explosive	3 min	3 x 4	3 x 4	3 x 6	3 x 6
E	Static Lunge	3/1/1	2 min	1 x 8, 1 x 6, 1 x 4	1 x 6, 1 x 6, 1 x 4	1 x 6, 1 x 6, 1 x 4	1 x 6, 1 x 4
F	Glute Ham Raise Greater reps/load may be used if proficient.	3/0/1	2 min	3 x 6	3 x 6	3 x 8	3 x 8

NB:
Borzov Jumps must be conducted on a forgiving surface such as a gym mat.

Two Days Olympic/Power (Beginner)

Prerequisites: Maximum strength/Hypertrophy, Advanced push pull, Intensification (4 day), 4 years' lifting experience plus technical coaching.

Synopsis: The use of Olympic lifts is well documented to be an effective modality for increasing lower body power production. However, its implementation requires significant technical experience. If using these lifts for the first time ensure qualified coaching is utilised to establish technique. Not suitable for anybody with lower limb or back injuries or disabilities. Suitable for individuals incorporating other training elements (fitness/speed, etc) into their weekly schedule.

Aim of program: Introductory Olympic lifts/power

Session 1 (MONDAY)

ORDER	EXERCISE	TEMPO	REC	WEEK 1	WEEK 2	WEEK 3	WEEK 4
A	Speed Shrug from Hang (Clean Grip)	Explosive	2 min	3 x 6	3 x 6	3 x 4	3 x 4
B	Speed Shrug from Floor (Clean Grip)	Explosive	3 min	3 x 4	3 x 4	3 x 3	3 x 3
C	Front Squat	3/2/1	3 min	3 x 8	3 x 8	3 x 6	3 x 6
D	Glute Ham Raise	2/1/1	2 min	2 x 6	2 x 6	2 x 6	2 x 6
E	Depth Drop Push-ups	Explosive	3 min	3 x 6 (2 plates)	3 x 6	3 x 4 (3 plates)	2 x 4
E	Single Arm Olympic Bar Row	3/1/1	90 sec	3 x 6	3 x 6	3 x 6	2 x 6
F	Dips	3/1/1	90 sec	3 x 6	3 x 6	3 x 6	2 x 6

NB:

■ Depth Drop Push-ups should be started using no more than 2 plates (as per picture and description on p 81). In the third week of the program increase the drop height to 3 plates and reduce the reps to 4. Should be conducted on a forgiving surface such as a gym mat.

■ Execution of Speed Shrug variations should be aimed at perfecting technique. Conservative increase in load expected at Week 3.

Session 2 (THURSDAY)

ORDER	EXERCISE	TEMPO	REC	WEEK 1	WEEK 2	WEEK 3	WEEK 4
A	Speed Shrug from Hang (Snatch Grip)	Explosive	2 min	3 x 6	3 x 6	3 x 4	3 x 4
B	Overhead Squat	3/1/1	3 min	3 x 8	3 x 8	3 x 6	2 x 6
C	Wide Grip Incline Bench Press	3/1/1	2 min	1 x 8, 1 x 6, 1 x 4	1 x 6, 1 x 6, 1 x 4	1 x 6, 1 x 4, 1 x 4	1 x 6, 1 x 4
D	Chin-ups UG	3/1/1	2 min	1 x 8, 1 x 6, 1 x 4	1 x 6, 1 x 6, 1 x 4	1 x 6, 1 x 6, 1 x 4	1 x 6, 1 x 4
E	Borzov Jump	Explosive	3 min	3 x 4	3 x 4	3 x 6	3 x 6
F	Good Morning	3/1/1	2 min	1 x 8, 1 x 6, 1 x 4	1 x 6, 1 x 6, 1 x 4	1 x 6, 1 x 6, 1 x 4	1 x 6, 1 x 4

NB:

■ Borzov Jumps must be conducted on a forgiving surface such as a gym mat.

■ Execution of Speed Shrug variations should be aimed at perfecting technique. Conservative increase in load expected at Week 3.

TRAIN TOUGH

Two Days Olympic/Power (Intermediate)

Prerequisites: Olympic/Power (beginner) Maximum strength/Hypertrophy, Intensification (4 day), 4 years' lifting experience plus technical coaching.

Synopsis: The use of Olympic lifts is well documented to be an effective modality for increasing lower body power production. However, its implementation requires significant technical experience. If using these lifts for the first time ensure qualified coaching is utilised to establish technique. Not suitable for anybody with lower limb or back injuries or disabilities. Suitable for individuals incorporating other training elements (fitness/speed, etc) into their weekly schedule.

Session 1 (MONDAY)

ORDER	EXERCISE	TEMPO	REC	WEEK 1	WEEK 2	WEEK 3	WEEK 4
A	Hang Clean + Front Squat	Explosive	2 min	3 x 6	3 x 6	3 x 4	3 x 4
B	Speed Shrug from Floor (Clean Grip)	Explosive	3 min	3 x 4	3 x 4	3 x 3	3 x 3
C	Front Squat	3/2/1	3 min	3 x 8	3 x 8	3 x 6	3 x 6
D	Glute Ham Raise	2/1/1	2 min	2 x 6	2 x 6	2 x 6	2 x 6
E	Depth Drop Push-ups	Explosive	3 min	3 x 6 (2 plates)	3 x 6	3 x 4 (3 plates)	2 x 4
E	Single Arm Olympic Bar Row	3/1/1	90 sec	3 x 6	3 x 6	3 x 6	2 x 6
F	Dips	3/1/1	90 sec	3 x 6	3 x 6	3 x 6	2 x 6

NB:

■ Depth Drop Push-ups should be started using no more than 2 plates (as per picture and description on p 81). In the third week of the program increase the drop height to 3 plates and reduce the reps to 4. Should be conducted on a forgiving surface such as a gym mat

■ Focus on technique development in Hang Clean + Front Squat, not weight.

■ Increase load for Speed Shrug from Floor compared to previous program.

Session 2 (THURSDAY)

ORDER	EXERCISE	TEMPO	REC	WEEK 1	WEEK 2	WEEK 3	WEEK 4
A	Hang Snatch + Overhead Squat	Explosive + 3/1/1	2 min	3 x 6	3 x 6	3 x 4	3 x 4
B	Speed Shrug from Floor (Snatch Grip)	Explosive	3 min	3 x 4	3 x 4	3 x 3	3 x 3
C	Reverse Grip Bench Press	3/1/1	2 min	1 x 8, 1 x 6, 1 x 4	1 x 6, 1 x 6, 1 x 4	1 x 6, 1 x 4, 1 x 4	1 x 6, 1x4
D	Chin-ups UG	3/1/1	2 min	1 x 8, 1 x 6, 1 x 4	1 x 6, 1 x 6, 1 x 4	1 x 6, 1 x 6, 1 x 4	1 x 6, 1 x 4
E	Single Leg Hitch	Explosive	3 min	3 x 4	3 x 4	3 x 6	3 x 6
F	Static Lunge	3/1/1	2 min	1 x 8, 1 x 6, 1 x 4	1 x 6, 1 x 6, 1 x 4	1 x 6, 1 x 6, 1 x 4	1 x 6, 1 x 4

TRAIN TOUGH

Two Days Olympic/Power (Advanced)
Prerequisites: Olympic/Power (intermediate) Maximum Strength/Hypertrophy, Intensification (4 day), 4 years' lifting experience plus technical coaching.

Synopsis: The use of Olympic lifts is well documented to be an effective modality for increasing lower body power production. However, its implementation requires significant technical experience. If using these lifts for the first time ensure qualified coaching is utilised to establish technique. Not suitable for anybody with lower limb or back injuries or disabilities. Suitable for individuals incorporating other training elements (fitness/speed, etc) into their weekly schedule.

Aim of program: Power

Session 1 (MONDAY)

ORDER	EXERCISE	TEMPO	REC	WEEK 1	WEEK 2	WEEK 3	WEEK 4
A	Power Clean	Explosive	2 min	4 x 3	4 x 3	4 x 2	4 x 2
B	Speed Shrug	Explosive	3 min	2 x 3	2 x 3	2 x 2	2 x 2
C	Front Squat	3/2/1	3 min	3 x 6	3 x 6	3 x 4	2 x 4
D	Good Morning	2/1/1	2 min	2 x 6	2 x 6	2 x 6	2 x 6
E	Depth Drop Push-ups (elevate feet)	Explosive	3 min	3 x 6 (2 plates)	3 x 6	3 x 4 (3 plates)	2 x 4
E	Single Arm Olympic Bar Row	3/1/1	90 sec	3 x 6	3 x 6	3 x 6	2 x 6
F	Dips	3/1/1	90 sec	3 x 6	3 x 6	3 x 6	2 x 6

NB:
- Depth Drop Push-ups should be started using no more than 2 plates (as per picture and description on p 81). In the third week of the program increase the drop height to 3 plates and reduce the reps to 4. Should be conducted on a forgiving surface such as a gym mat.

Session 2 (THURSDAY)

ORDER	EXERCISE	TEMPO	REC	WEEK 1	WEEK 2	WEEK 3	WEEK 4
A	Power Snatch	Explosive	2 min	4 x 3	4 x 3	4 x 2	4 x 2
B	Speed Shrug from Floor (Snatch Grip)	Explosive	3 min	2 x 3	2 x 3	2 x 2	2 x 2
C	Close Grip Bench Press	3/1/1	2 min	1 x 8, 1 x 6, 1 x 4	1 x 6, 1 x 6, 1 x 4	1 x 6, 1 x 4, 1 x 4	1 x 6, 1 x 4
D	Chin-ups Mixed Grip	3/1/1	2 min	1 x 8, 1 x 6, 1 x 4	1 x 6, 1 x 6, 1 x 4	1 x 6, 1 x 6, 1 x 4	1 x 6, 1 x 4
E	Single Leg Hitch	Explosive	3 min	3 x 4	3 x 4	3 x 6	3 x 6
F	Dynamic Lunge	3/1/1	2 min	1 x 8, 1 x 6, 1 x 4	1 x 6, 1 x 6, 1 x 4	1 x 6, 1 x 6, 1 x 4	1 x 6, 1 x 4

TRAIN TOUGH

Two Days Olympic/Power — 'Something a Little Different'

Prerequisites: Olympic/Power (advanced) Maximum Strength/Hypertrophy, Intensification (4 day), 4 years lifting experience plus technical coaching.

Synopsis: This program contains exercises that are extremely challenging and should be implemented is association with qualified coaching. Not suitable for anybody with lower limb or back injuries or disabilities. Suitable for the individuals incorporating other training elements (fitness/speed etc) into their weekly schedule.

Aim of program: Power

Session 1 (MONDAY)

ORDER	EXERCISE	TEMPO	REC	WEEK 1	WEEK 2	WEEK 3	WEEK 4
A	Single Arm DB Snatch	Explosive	2 min	4 x 6	4 x 6	4 x 4	3 x 4
B	Borzov Jump	Explosive	3 min	2 x 4	2 x 4	2 x 4	2 x 4
C	Dynamic Lunge	3/2/1	3 min	3 x 6	3 x 6	3 x 4	2 x 4
D	Single Arm Squat & Reach	2/1/1	2 min	2 x 6	2 x 6	2 x 6	2 x 6
E	2 Clap Push-up	Explosive	3 min	3 x 4	3 x 4	3 x 6	2 x 6
E	Single Arm Olympic Bar Row	3/1/1	90 sec	3 x 6	3 x 6	3 x 6	2 x 6
F	Dips	3/1/1	90 sec	3 x 6	3 x 6	3 x 6	2 x 6

Session 2 (THURSDAY)

ORDER	EXERCISE	TEMPO	REC	WEEK 1	WEEK 2	WEEK 3	WEEK 4
A	Single Arm Snatch	Explosive	2 min	4 x 3	4 x 3	4 x 2	4 x 2
B	Hang Snatch	Explosive	3 min	2 x 3	2 x 3	2 x 2	2 x 2
C	Close Grip Bench Press	3/1/1	2 min	1 x 8, 1 x 6, 1 x 4	1 x 6, 1 x 6, 1 x 4	1 x 6, 1 x 4, 1 x 4	1 x 6, 1 x 4
D	Chin-ups Mixed Grip	3/1/1	2 min	1 x 8, 1 x 6, 1 x 4	1 x 6, 1 x 6, 1 x 4	1 x 6, 1 x 6, 1 x 4	1 x 6, 1 x 4
E	Exchange Jump	Explosive	3 min	3 x 4	3 x 4	3 x 6	3 x 6
F	Dynamic Lunge	3/1/1	2 min	1 x 8, 1 x 6, 1 x 4	1 x 6, 1 x 6, 1 x 4	1 x 6, 1 x 6, 1 x 4	1 x 6, 1 x 4

NB:
- Single Arm Snatch: if not confident using Olympic Bar, use DB.

14 SEALED SECTION

The aim of this chapter is to give more advanced lifters ideas on how to add variables to their programs to achieve superior results.

METHODS OF APPLYING RESISTANCE TRAINING

After decades of massive government support of elite athletic programs, Eastern Bloc countries have contributed great volumes of knowledge to the development of advanced strength levels. During the later stages of the USSR, many sports scientists moved to the US, taking up residence at leading universities and unveiling the secrets of Eastern Bloc athletic domination.

Former Russian sport scientist and leading author Vladimir Zatsiorsky described in his landmark text *Science & Practice of Strength Training* three methods of lifting which contribute to differing areas of strength, yet each can be used in combination.

Maximum Effort Method (MEM)

As the name suggests, Maximum Effort Method refers to the exposure of the body to training loads which create maximal contraction of the targeted muscle groups. For advanced strength trainers the most important variable is intensity and use of this methodology provides one of the greatest sources of intensity. For example:

- ■ Bench Press
  - Warm up: 1 x 6 @ 60%, 1 x 6 @ 70%
  - 1 x 4 @ 80%
  - 1 x 1 @ 95%
  - 1 x 2 @ 80%
  - 1 x 1 @ 97.5%
  - 1 x 1 @ 100%

> The need to increase training loads and progress towards maximal loading is based on the thesis that physical loads, which are most capable of significantly disrupting homeostasis, elicit the greatest training effect.
>
> Mel Siff (*Super Training* 1999)
> This text was written by legendary sport scientists Mel Siff & Yuri Verkhoshansky
> (refer to Training Resources on p 214)

Dynamic Effort Method (DEM)

Dynamic Effort Method is the application of moderately high resistance lifted at the maximum speed possible. This form of loading is very effective at increasing the rate of force development or RFD (power) in the chosen exercise. Greater application of power allows the inertia (resistance to change of motion) of an object to be overcome more rapidly, thus increasing the momentum (mass x velocity) of the bar in the direction we want it to go. A bar moving with greater momentum will meet less resistance at the point of least mechanical efficiency (the sticking point) and therefore be able to blast through previous barriers. For example:

- Bench Press 8 x 3 @ 70% on 60 sec
  NB: a new set must start every minute, that is, 10 sec lift, 50 sec recovery (don't leave a minute between each set).

- This lifting methodology is a phenomenal adjunct to the MEM.

- It can also be used as a short cycle by itself. Use for 2 to 3 weeks as a 'change up' to a conventional program.

- The resistance can be varied for different effect (minimum resistance 60%, maximum resistance 80%).

- DEM lifts are typically employed in conjunction with MEM lifts in the following manner (reminiscent of the Westside Barbell Method):
  - Monday: DEM upper body
  - Tuesday: MEM lower body
  - Friday: MEM upper body
  - Saturday: DEM lower body

TECHNICAL TIP
Westside Barbell Club under the direction of Louie Simmons have all but perfected the integration of the Maximal Effort Method and Dynamic Effort Method within the sport of powerlifting. For more detailed information on this training methodology refer directly to the Westside Barbell website (refer to Training Resources on p 214).

Repeated Effort Method (REM)
For the most part, the programs in *Train tough* reflect the Repeated Effort Method of lifting. This involves applying less than maximal load on a muscle group and lifting it a number of times in succession for the purpose of disrupting the homeostatic environment of the muscle and stimulating muscle hypertrophy. While this works well for increasing general strength it will not allow the individual to explore the limits of his potential. For example:

- Bench Press 4 x 6 @ 75%

Identifying the three methods of applying resistance as detailed by Zatsiorsky illustrates another twist in the possibilities for variety in strength training.

TRICKS OF THE TRADE
The techniques detailed below are intended to allow the individual to identify new elements that he may add to his program in order to improve weak links in the chain.

Restricted range lifts
Every lift has what is colloquially known as a sticking point. This is the point of least mechanical efficiency in a movement. There are primarily two ways to get through the sticking point with more efficiency:

1 Hit the sticking point at a greater speed. This requires greater power in the bottom position to accelerate the load faster (see Dynamic Effort Method above).

2 Specifically train the ability to apply greater force at the sticking point, so that when the load slows (as it does for everybody no matter how powerful they are) you can apply greater force and 'muscle out' the last section of the lift.

The use of restricted range lifts can assist in the development of greater strength in the outer range of a lift. This method is best applied to core lifts such as Squat and Bench Press. Partial lifts, while good, should only be used as an adjunct to the full lifts they are related too. (By that I mean you should not brag about your half-squat ability.)

NERD MOMENT

While some of you may have looked down on those geeky guys at school who studied physics and maths, it's the information learned in those classes that dramatically influences the methodology of lifting. Understanding some basic principles of physics contributes to better understanding of what you are trying to do.

Most of this stuff is borrowed from a little known English powerlifter, Sir Isaac Newton.

Inertia is the property of matter that causes it to resist any change to its motion in either direction or speed. *The First Law of Motion* accurately describes this property: an object at rest tends to remain at rest, and an object in motion tends to continue in motion in a straight line, unless acted upon by an outside force. Changing the direction an object is moving in or the speed at which it is moving requires application of force. The stronger you are the greater the force you can apply, hence the greater your ability to dictate the direction in which an object will travel.

The Second Law of Motion states that the force acting on a body in motion must be equal to its rate of change of momentum. That is, the acceleration must be proportional to the magnitude of the force and in the same direction as the force. The faster the force that can be applied (that is, the application of power) the greater the acceleration that can be achieved therefore making it possible to crack those annoying sticking points (see above in Tricks of the Trade).

The Third Law of Motion states that for every action there is an equal and opposite reaction. This law's application to lifting goes like this: as you apply force to the bar in order to move it, so the bar applies the same force to you. Therefore your base of support must be extremely strong and stable, be it in a standing, seated or lying position, and refers to both your body and your equipment.

Floor Press

Executed exactly the same as for conventional bench press with the exception that lying on the floor will restrict the range of movement. The focus of the exercise is to emphasise loading on the top end of the range of motion.

Other variations on this theme include:

- Pin Press: Using the pins in a power rack, set the bottom position for the press. This height may be used as another variable within the exercise.

- Board Press (Westside favourite): Have your training partner hold between 1–4 20 mm boards on your chest during the Bench Press to restrict the range of movement.

Half Squats

As the name suggests the Squat is executed to only halfway of the range of movement. As for the Pin Press, pins in a power rack may be used to set the range of movement.

For a great general preparation variation try:

- Squats: Take the bar as for a conventional Squat. Squat all the way to the bottom position, pause then return up to halfway, return to the bottom position and then finish by returning to the start position for the completion of one rep.

Run the Rack

This technique may be used with any exercise that uses dumbbells. It is in essence a Strip (or Drop) Set in which you lift as heavy as you can in the first set and then progressively lighten the load over successive sets. The theory is that you recruit the highest threshold (fast twitch) fibres first, fatiguing them and then continue to load the muscle, producing a cascading fatigue as you progress down in weight. This subjects as many muscle fibres as possible to fatigue and therefore the potential to adapt.

For example:
DB Shrugs (listed below in the Double Split program)

Set 1: 1 x 6 @ 40 kg
Set 2: 1 x 6 @ 35 kg
Set 3: 1 x 6 @ 30 kg
Set 4: 1 x 6 @ 20 kg
Repeat 2 to 3 times.

- Go in easy the first time as this tends to blow people away.

- Works well with exercises like Curls (any variant), DB Shoulder Press, DB Bench Press.

- Strip Sets work in much the same way with the exception that the weight is typically taken off the bar as you are completing exercises like Squat, Bench Press and so on.

TRAIN TOUGH

Using cluster sets and evolving density to improve body weight exercises

For many people the prospect of completing a set of Chin-ups is the most daunting element to a training program. This is with good reason: they're among the toughest exercises to complete. Not everybody is gifted with the ability to jump straight in and start cranking out multiple sets of chins. So how do you generate progress in an exercise when you can't even do one rep in the first place? Read on young Jedi...

By the completion of the final step you'll have done as many as 32 Chin-ups in a session and be ready to complete any conventional program, including those that use external resistance, such as carrying extra weight while you chin the bar.

Chin-ups

1   If you can't complete four reps in one set you are better off developing a greater level of basic strength before attempting Chin-ups as an independent element. Use this program as a starting point (if you can do four Chin-ups move to step two).

EXERCISES	WEEK 1–2	WEEK 3–4	WEEK 5–6
Overhand Grip Pull Ups (maintain strong body position, bring chest to the bar)	4 x 10 (try to sustain the same load through all sets)	4 x 8 (increase the load from the previous week and try to maintain in all sets)	4 x 6 (increase the load from the previous week and try to maintain in all sets)
Underhand Grip Pull Downs (push chest out to meet the bar)	3 x 10 (try to sustain the same load through all sets)	3 x 8 (increase the load from the previous week and try to maintain in all sets)	3 x 6 (increase the load from the previous week and try to maintain in all sets)

NB:
Use small numbers of repetitions in multiple sets, over time building the reps and sets to increase the total volume you can sustain.

EXERCISES	WEEK 1–2	WEEK 3–4	WEEK 5–6
Underhand Grip Chin-up	5–6 sets of 2 reps 90 sec between sets	5–6 sets of 3 reps 90 sec between reps	5–6 sets of 4 reps 90 sec between reps

2 Begin to reduce the recovery between reps in order to increase the density of each set.

EXERCISES	WEEK 1–2	WEEK 3–4	WEEK 5–6
Underhand Grip Chin-up	4 sets of (3 x 2 reps with 10 sec recovery) 90 sec between sets	4 sets of (3 x 3 reps with 10 sec recovery) 90 sec between sets	4 sets of (3 x 4 reps with 10 sec recovery) 90 sec between sets

3 The final step is to build greater volume in individual sets.

EXERCISES	WEEK 1–2	WEEK 3–4	WEEK 5–6
Underhand Grip Chin-up	3–4 sets of 6 reps	3–4 sets of 7 reps	3–4 sets of 8 reps

Double Split ... only the brave

For the purposes of bodybuilding, the benefit of using a split system lies in being able to apply a greater volume of lifts to the entire body in the space of a week. For those who are crazy enough to try it, the Double Split serves to amplify the effect of high volume training even further by completing two weeks' training in one, and then backing the whole program up two weeks in a row. Sounds ridiculous but it works!

Because of the extreme nature of the loading this program requires, enormous amounts of recovery work is required. It's suggested this program only be attempted when you can commit to two weeks of absolutely selfish behaviour. Tell your partner, your friends, your parole officer, whoever, that you will be off the radar for the duration of this program. If you choose not to follow the recovery guidelines as diligently as you follow the training guidelines then *you will fail*.

This system is fantastic for putting on weight quickly, busting training plateaus and increasing overall work capacity. There are, however, some very important rules that *must* be adhered to or the whole program will be a farce.

They are:

1 Only lifters with a minimum of 5 years experience should attempt this program.

2 *Eat, sleep, shit, lift.* This is the tenet of the Double Split program. Do not plan any significant extra curricular activities while attempting this program.

3 Every session must be preceded by a light meal and/or protein supplementation.

4 Every session must be followed by a light meal and/or protein supplementation.

5   Five to 6 balanced meals must be consumed every day with additional fluid nutrition if required.

6   Every session must be followed by a minimum of 30 min sleep.

7   Aim for a minimum of 10 hr sleep overnight.

8   Do not attempt this program if you are carrying any injuries!

9   This program should not be extended beyond the scheduled two-week training block as significant overtraining issues may arise.

Remember: this program is a specialised training mechanism. It's designed only as a short training stimulus. For most people this will barely be tolerable for two weeks – don't try to extend it! This is definitely a situation where more is not better. Some individuals may find they need a week off after it. There's nothing wrong with that, but a standard 3 to 4 day per week program should be initiated straight after the break.

Session 1 (MONDAY AM)

ORDER	EXERCISE	TEMPO	REC	WEEK 1	WEEK 2
A	UG Chin-up	3/1/1	90 sec	3 x 5	3 x 6
B	OH Grip Pulldown	4/2/1	90 sec	4 x 6	4 x 8
C1	Reverse DB Flys	3/1/1	N/A	3 x 12	3 x 10
C2	Seated Row	3/1/1	90 sec	3 x 12	3 x 8
D1	DB Lat. Raise	2/0/1	N/A	3 x 12	2 x 8, 1 x 12
D2	Upright Row	2/1/1	90 sec	3 x 12	2 x 8, 1 x 12

Session 2 (MONDAY PM)

ORDER	EXERCISE	TEMPO	REC	WEEK 1	WEEK 2
A	Bench Press	2/1/X	90 sec	2 x 6 @80%	2 x 4 @ 85%
B	Bench Press (Slow)	4/2/1	90 sec	4 x 6	4 x 6
C1	DB Flys	2/0/1	N/A	4 x 12	4 x 10
C2	Incline DB Press	3/1/1	90 sec	4 x 12	4 x 8
D	DB Shoulder Press	4/2/1	90 sec	4 x 6	4 x 6

SESSION 3 (TUESDAY AM)

ORDER	EXERCISE	TEMPO	REC	WEEK 1	WEEK 2
A	90 degree Squat	3/1/1	90 sec	2 x 6 @ 90%	2 x 6 @ 90%
B	Parallel Squat	4/1/1	90 sec	2 x 8 @ 75%	2 x 8 @ 75%
C	Full Squat	5/1/1	90 sec	2 x10@ 60%	2 x 10@ 60%
D1	Romanian Deadlift	4/1/1	N/A	3 x 6	3 x 6
D2	Single Leg Calf Raise	2/2/2	90 sec	3 x 15	3 x 15
E	Back Extension	3/1/1	90 sec	3 x 12	3 x 12
F	Single Leg Lying Ham Curl	4/1/1	90 sec	2 x 8	2 x 8

SESSION 4 (TUESDAY PM)

ORDER	EXERCISE	TEMPO	REC	WEEK 1	WEEK 2
A1	Snatch Grip Shrug	2/2/2	N/A	3 x 12	3 x 8
A2	DB Shrug Run the Rack	2/2/2	90 sec	3 x (4 x 6)	3 x (4 x 6)
C	CG Bench Press	3/1/1	90 sec	4 x 12	4 x 8
D1	Decline Tricep Ext.	2/1/1	N/A	3 x 12	3 x 8
D2	DB Hammer Press	2/1/1	90 sec	3 x 12	3 x 8
E	Standing EZY Bar Matrix Curl	Slow	90 sec	4 x 5's	4 x 5's

SESSION 5 (THURSDAY AM)

ORDER	EXERCISE	TEMPO	REC	WEEK 1	WEEK 2
A	3 Way Upright Row (wide, medium, close grip)	2/1/1	90 sec	4 x 6 @ each grip	4 x 4 @ each grip
B	DB Lat. Raise Run the Rack	2/0/1	90 sec	3 x (4 x 4)	3 x (4 x 4)
C	OH Grip Chin Up	3/1/1	90 sec	3 x 6	3 x 8
D	UH Grip Pulldown	4/2/1	90 sec	3 x 12	3 x 8
E	Bent Over Row OH	2/0/1	90 sec	3 x 12	3 x 8

TRAIN TOUGH

SESSION 6 (THURSDAY PM)

ORDER	EXERCISE	TEMPO	REC	WEEK 1	WEEK 2
A	Military Press	4/2/1	90 sec	4 x 6	4 x 6
B	DB Shoulder Press	2/1/1	90 sec	4 x 8	4 x 8
C	Behind Neck Press	2/1/1	90 sec	2 x 12	2 x 12
D1	DB Flys	2/0/1	N/A	3 x 12	3 x 10
D2	Incline DB Press	2/1/1	90 sec	3 x 10	3 x 8
E	Wide Grip Bench Press	2/1/1	90 sec	2 x 12	2 x 8

SESSION 7 (FRIDAY AM)

ORDER	EXERCISE	TEMPO	REC	WEEK 1	WEEK 2
A	Split Squat	3/1/1	90 sec	4 x 12	4 x 8
B	Leg Press	4/1/1	90 sec	4 x 12	4 x 8
C1	Romanian Deadlift	4/1/1	N/A	3 x 6	3 x 6
C2	Single Leg Calf Raise	2/2/2	90 sec	3 x 15	3 x 15
D	Back Extension	3/1/1	90 sec	3 x 12	3 x 12
E	Single Leg Squat & Reach	4/1/1	90 sec	2 x 12	2 x 12

SESSION 8 (FRIDAY PM)

ORDER	EXERCISE	TEMPO	REC	WEEK 1	WEEK 2
A1	Snatch Shrug	2/2/2	N/A	3 x 12	3 x 8
A2	DB Shrug Run the Rack	2/2/2	90 sec	3 x (4 x 6)	3 x (4 x 6)
C	CG Bench Press	3/1/1	90 sec	4 x 12	4 x 8
D1	Dips	3/2/1	N/A	3 x 12	3 x 8
D2	DB Hammer Press	2/1/1	90 sec	3 x 12	3 x 8
E	Standing EZY Bar Matrix Curl	Slow	90 sec	4 x 5's	4 x 5's

Extreme Cycle

This program adds extra grunt to the cycles in Chapter 8, 'Foundation Training'. Do not treat it lightly – ensure you have built up your performance base through all the other cycles. Use it once per week in conjunction with the Advanced Cycle (see pp 114–115).

E I

EXERCISE	NOTES	WEEK 1	WEEK 2	WEEK 3	WEEK 4
Round The World	Start with 10 kg and progress up slowly	3 x 5 each way	3 x 7 each way (use same load from week 1)	3 x 5 each way (increase load from week 2)	3 x 7 each way (use same load as week 3)
Hanging Lateral Knee Raise		2 x 8	2 x 10	2 x 12	2 x 14
Dragon Slayer	Add load via med-ball. Stay strict.	2 x 6 (approx 2 kg ball)	2 x 8 (approx 2 kg ball)	2 x 6 (approx 4 kg ball)	2 x 8 (approx 4 kg ball)
Olympic Bar Laterals	Increase load, maintaining strict technique	2 x 8	2 x 10 (use same load as week 1)	2 x 8 (increase load from week 2)	2 x 10 (use same load as week 3)
Med-ball Juggle	Start with balls approx 4 to 5 kg	2 x 30 sec	2 x 45 sec (use same load as week 1)	2 x 30 sec (increase load from week 2)	2 x 45 sec (use same load as week 3)

15. TRAINING JOURNAL

One of the keys to continuing success in your training is unquestionably your training journal. While it may seem a bit of overkill for the average athlete, it is one of the pillars of a solid program.

A training journal serves several key functions:

- Gives you a concrete and accessible way to commit your goals to something other than the whisper of a passing thought.

- Writing your program in a journal before training allows you to review your current plans and goals and keeps you on track.

- Allows you the ability to review training sessions to ensure that you are progressing.

- Gives you the satisfaction of seeing how far you have come with your training.

Keeping a training journal is simple. You only need to buy a pencil and a small diary or blank notebook.

I've seen the training journals of a number of Olympic gold medalists and they all record a similar quality of information but write it down in different ways. One athlete showed what they were feeling in terms of emotion and fatigue using angry faces and dark colours, while another's writing fell apart (not to mention the expletives). Similarly, on good days one athlete drew roses, sunshine and used bright colours, while the other had incredibly beautiful writing.

Let your journal reflect you and enjoy it.

Recording your training doesn't require you to think like a brain surgeon. Simply write down information for each element of your session.

For example:

Set 1: Squat 10/100 8/110 6/120 6/125 6/125 with 10/100 meaning 10 reps @ 100 kg

Set 2:	Rowing Erg	60 sec	310 m
		60 sec	305 m
		60 sec	302 m

TRAINING TIP

- Don't forget to record the day and date for easy reference.

- Make a few notes about how you feel as it will give you feedback on how you are recovering within the program.

If you are keen to make the reviewing process easier you can use a spreadsheet program on your computer to track performance.

Sample structure (developed using Microcoft Excel)

	Date	Day	Session Type	Exercise	Session Content
	Date	**Day**	**Session Type**	**Exercise**	**Session Content**
3	21/02/2005	Monday	Aerobic	Rowing	10 x 60sec on/off - average distance 310m
4	22/02/2005	Tuesday	Aerobic	Run	Point A - B - C 38:67
5	23/02/2005	Wednesday	Strength	Squat	10/60 10/80 6/110 6/120 6/120
6	23/02/2005	Wednesday	Strength	Bench Press	8/90 6/100 4/102 4/102
7	23/02/2005	Wednesday	Strength	Chin Up UG	6/BW +10 x 3
8	25/02/2005	Friday	Aerobic	Run	Point A - B - C 35:23
9	27/02/2005	Sunday	Strength	Deadlift	6/120 6/130 4/150 4/155
10	27/02/2005	Sunday	Strength	Squat	10/60 10/80 6/110 6/125 6/130
11	27/02/2005	Sunday	Strength	Bench Press	8/90 6/100 4/107.5 4/110
12	27/02/2005	Sunday	Strength	Bent Over Row OH	4/80 x 4

JOURNAL TIPS

■ Set columns out as above. Columns are essentially the elements you will use to search, so include as many as you think you need.

■ Session content may be recorded in any manner you choose, but be consistent as you want to be able to compare similar sessions.

■ You can record as few or as many strength exercises as you like. As a minimum record the fundamental lifts, and as a maximum the sky is the limit.

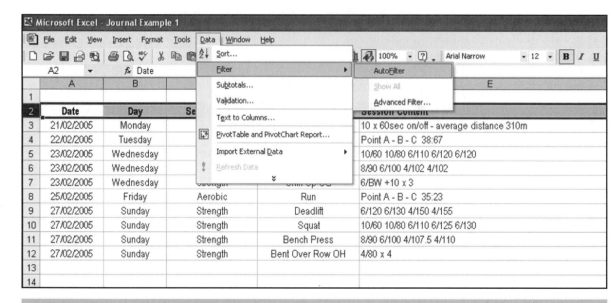

JOURNAL TIPS – REVIEWING PERFORMANCE

■ Select the variables row, then Data, Filter, Auto filter.

■ The Auto Filter will be highlighted on each variable allowing you to select which element you wish to look at within that variable eg: all sessions on a specific date, every time you have done Squat, every run you have done etc. (see below).

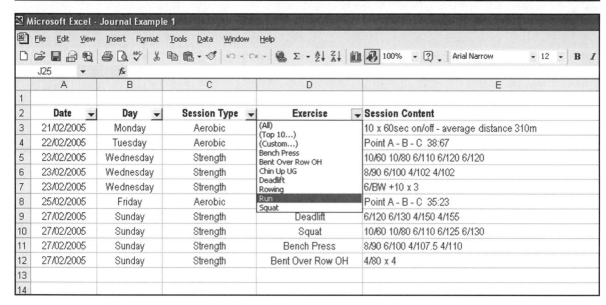

	A	B	C	D	E
1					
2	**Date** ▾	**Day** ▾	**Session Type** ▾	**Exercise** ▾	**Session Content**
4	22/02/2005	Tuesday	Aerobic	Run	Point A - B - C 38:67
8	25/02/2005	Friday	Aerobic	Run	Point A - B - C 35:23
13					
14					
15					
16					
17					
18					
19					
20					

Microsoft Excel - Journal Example 1

JOURNAL TIPS – REVIEWING PERFORMANCE

■ The Auto Filter allows you to look one element of training in detail eg Run in the above example.

■ You may have four different runs that you do regularly – under Exercise name them as Run 1–4 then you can compare each of them directly over time.

The Auto Filter will be highlighted on each variable allowing you to select which element you wish to look at within.

The examples above are very straightforward forms of data basing. In the world of data management this is a massive area. You can use this method as a base line and develop more advanced skills using some of the other features of the software you use.

Remember that the key to success is to keep a record of where you have been so that you can be definite about where you are going.

16 TRAINING RESOURCES

Throughout the writing of *Train Tough* I have been continually challenged by my editor to keep the message simple and user-friendly for the average recreational athlete. Hopefully, too, some of what I've said will have stimulated the curious among you to search out more detail in regards to some of the more advanced methodologies briefly touched upon.

This section mentions a number of the various resources that I utilise on a regular basis to both keep up to speed and challenge my thinking.

The sites detailed below are ones that I regularly have a look at. Some of the information on these sites is aimed at extremely high level athletes, so be aware when attempting to use that information that you may need to spend some more time on developing your training base before you get stuck in.

http://www.elitefts.com/

This is a fantastic site that lives and breathes the Westside Barbell training methodology. It contains a ton of articles and an excellent range of equipment and resources that can be reliably sent internationally. The foundation for this site is based on competitive powerlifting and the content reflects this. The evolution of the methodologies described on this site is based on the work of some of the most respected sport scientists in the world and, as such, they are very sound in their logic.

http://www.inno-sport.net/

This site provides some real challenges to those who think they've got their heads around the basics. Some of the theories espoused by the site mastermind, Dietrich Buchenholz, challenge many current theories (both accepted and progressive) within strength and conditioning. That said, if you can wade through the unique terminologies, the

INTERNET WARNING

Anybody in the world (given the appropriate resources) can author a website. It doesn't take qualifications or significant experience to jot down your thoughts and publish on the internet. Be careful when surfing the web for strength and conditioning info as there are any number of twits out there who don't have a clue about what they are writing. Check the credentials of any site you visit if you have a mind to try to implement the material on their site.

advanced coach/athlete will find plenty to sink their teeth into. Be mindful that much of the content on this site will contradict information presented elsewhere … but that's the point, isn't it!

http://www.coachesinfo.com/
A plethora of articles providing in-depth information about a wide variety of sports.

http://www.strengthcats.com/
This site provides a variety of resources aimed at a wide spectrum of readers. A lot of the articles are based on the training regimens of fire fighters in the US. Plenty of articles from a range of authors … dig a little and you will find the quality ones.

http://westside-barbell.com/
The original and the best! Site master Louie Simmons developed the Westside Barbell training system through blood-soaked trial and error based on much of the work of Russian sport science great Vladimir Zatsiorsky. Louie provides a cornucopia of information on this site that could take the average reader weeks to get through. Again, it is founded on the competitive powerlifting scene and is primarily aimed at that market.

http://www.regenerationlab.com/
Provides a number of solid articles that give an intriguing view of a variety of recovery method. Will challenge the thinking of many recreational and professional athletes who think having a sugar-loaded drink and a 2 min stretch is all that is needed to recover from a session. Worth a look!

If you are looking to learn more about the functional management and prevention of back-related problems, this is the place to go:
Fix Your Back, Anna-Louise Bouvier, ABC Books
Physiocise Movement for Muscles Pty Ltd
Suite 14, 77 Penshurst St Willoughby,
Sydney, NSW 2068
Ph 02 9958 2239
Available from ABC shops and centres and leading retailers.
email: physiocise@tpg.com.au
website: www.physiocise.com.au

Profile Health Services
www.profilehealthservices.com
This company provides a wide variety of rehabilitation and muscle maintenance tools that can assist in returning athletes to sport quickly, and keep them there longer.

For the very keen here are a couple of books worth chasing up.

Science & Practice of Strength Training
Vladimir Zatsiorsky, Human Kinetics 1995

Super Training
Mel Siff & Yuri Verkhoshansky, Supertraining International 1999

Textbook of Work Physiology
Astrand & Rodahl, McGraw-Hill Book Co. 1986

17 ABBREVIATIONS

Suffering from a touch of CRA Syndrome (Can't Remember the Abbreviation)? Here's a list that might bring relief. Read them carefully before hitting the programs.

AT	anaerobic threshhold		**MG**	medium grip
ATP	adenosine triphosphate		**MHR**	maximum heart rate
BPM	beats per minute		**NG**	narrow grip
CG	close grip		**OG**	overhand grip
DB	dumb-bells		**REM**	repeated effort method
DEM	dynamic effort method		**REPS**	repetitions
ES	erector spinae		**RFD**	rate of force development
F	bar pulled to the front of the body		**RM**	repetition maximum
FIT	fitness training session		**RPM**	reps per minute
FT	fast twitch		**ST**	slow twitch
FTS	fusion training session		**STR**	strength training session
GPP	general physical preparation		**TB**	therapeutic ball
HR	heart rate		**UG**	underhand grip
LSD	long slow distance		**WG**	wide grip
MEM	maximum effort method		**XTR**	cross-training